Flirting

How to Flirt for Women Wanting to Date a High-Value Man, Including Seductive Body Language Techniques and a Guide to Get Your Ex Back

Contents

Part 1: Flirting for Women

The Ultimate Guide on How to Flirt Like Cleopatra and Use Non-Verbal Communication and Seduction Techniques to Start Dating High-Value Men

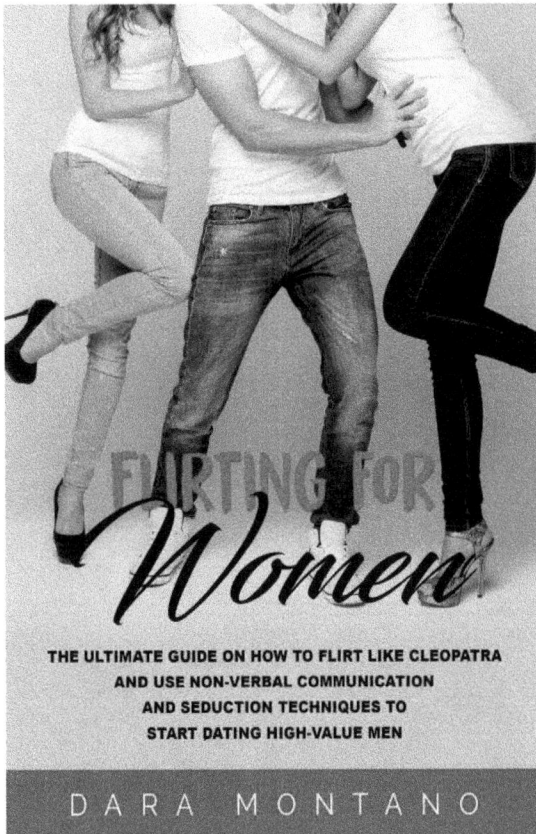

FLIRTING FOR

Women

THE ULTIMATE GUIDE ON HOW TO FLIRT LIKE CLEOPATRA
AND USE NON-VERBAL COMMUNICATION
AND SEDUCTION TECHNIQUES TO
START DATING HIGH-VALUE MEN

DARA MONTANO

Introduction

Everyone flirts, but some people are better at it than others. Flirting has a lot of benefits if you do it correctly. For instance, a person can get out of difficult situations by flirting his or her way out. Women are experts at flirting, but due to the rapidly changing world, many women have lost their edge in the world of flirting; that does not mean that these edges cannot be *sharpened!* This guide is sure to help women who want to practice and hone their flirting skills.

This book is a great guide for everyone. Even if you are new to the world of flirting, you will learn a lot from this book. It does not matter whether you have flirted before or not; this book will help everyone who wants to learn to flirt.

There are many different books related to flirting and seduction available on the market; they are quite popular as well. The one in your hands stands out from all the other books because, along with experts, many experienced and "qualified" flirters have collaborated in the book, making it highly readable and simple to understand. It is up-to-date and has a lot of new tricks, techniques, and strategies that you can use to flirt with your date; this book can work wonders for a woman who needs a little help with flirting.

Chapter One: Understanding Men and How They Really Think

Men – and many women - believe that women are complex and complicated creatures who are difficult, if not impossible, to understand. Still, many people realize that men are complex too. Decoding their minds and psyches is necessary for understanding them.

Due to the unfortunate stereotypes perpetuated about gender, men and women often have misunderstandings, believing some untrue myths about each other. Demystifying these myths can help both men and women to understand the dynamics of the society in a better way. In this section, let's look at how men think about women. This chapter specifically focuses on some of the most common misguided notions that men have about women, providing useful information about how to reassure men while flirting.

Fortune

Many men think that women love money, luxury, and that they are obsessed with material possessions. Everyone loves material pleasure, but only a few are "hooked" on it. It is not a common fixation. In fact, many women tend to avoid men whose main fixation in life is money and material wealth. Women care for men's passion, work ethics, hobbies, and ambition, more than how rich they are. This approach is seen in other factors too. If a man or woman is interested in only talking about money, then it is better to avoid dating them at all.

Physique

Another common myth that men associate with women is that they are obsessed with men with perfect and highly chiseled bodies. Most women find extremely buff guys off-putting or intimidating. They find these men judgmental and vain as well. No one likes to be self-conscious, and men in great physical shape can make women self-conscious. Similarly, no woman will appreciate it if her man spends more time at the gym instead of spending time with her. Caring about one's appearance is important - but not for the sake of others.

Size of Your Manhood

This is one of the most rampant myths that men associate with women. Most women do not care about the size of your penis, so the concept that "bigger is better" is just a myth. Penile size has become a benchmark for the masculine ego, but almost all penis sizes are acceptable (and enjoyable) for women. Your penis size says nothing about you or your personality, and certainly does not confirm your sexual potency and prowess. The only thing it does confirm is that you have a *big appendage between your legs!* Many men tend to develop self-confidence issues due to their penis size – a dastardly side effect of pornography and "big phallocentric" media culture. Women are more concerned about your personality and your attitude in bed - as well as outside of the bed. They care if you are an attentive and giving lover. They would prefer you to be with a man with a small penis - but a lot of techniques and passion - rather than dealing with a man with a giant penis, but zero understanding of pleasure.

Vulnerability

Vulnerability is another aspect that men think that women think is disgusting and unsexy. Many men even believe it to be unmanly as well. Showing appropriate emotions and feelings at appropriate times and situations is crucial for emotional health, physical health, and mental stability. Women love men who are in touch with their emotional side, men who can express their feelings without being uncomfortable. Men believe that women will judge them if they display their feelings in an obvious manner, but women find it sexy when men can display their emotions.

Women love men who are emotionally stable. This means that women love men who can cry while watching a sad movie and can display their emotions in appropriate situations. This does not mean that the man should go around moping and crying all the time, but true vulnerability shows ingenuity.

Putting Them on a Pedestal

Nobody in this world is perfect, and nobody likes to be treated like a god or goddess all the time. People like to enjoy the simple pleasures of life, which often come from hardships. Everyone has flaws, and these flaws need to be addressed, but many men believe that women love to be perfect, which is why they tend to put women on a pedestal and shower them with compliments day and night. A few compliments in the right situations and on the right occasions are good, but bombarding women with compliments makes men seem insincere. It often leads to disconnection and disconcertion in the relationship. Women do not like to be worshipped.

Women prefer having a connection with their men. Women love to be treated as equals. No one likes to be treated as superior or as inferior in any relationship; so, keeping up the idealized version and its façade can be quite difficult in the long term. This often leads to the formation of cracks in a relationship, and ultimately, the relationship falters.

Superficiality

Men believe that complimenting women about their looks all the time is the best way to flirt with them. This is obviously untrue. Women like being complimented about their looks, but if a man can think only about one thing worth complimenting them about, then the whole relationship becomes old and clichéd very soon. In fact, it also becomes demeaning, because it shows that your man does not understand that you are much more than your looks.

Men understand that there are many things worth complimenting and noticing about their women, but they are afraid to bring them up because they believe that women will not appreciate it. Women can help their men in such cases by reassuring them and projecting their relationship from an optimistic point of view.

Vanity

Men and women alike believe that women are vainer than men, but this is a myth. Men have been vain since ancient times! Men care a lot about their appearances, especially their hairline, their graying hair, etc. Instead of spending a lot of time on improving appearance, men should concentrate on improving their personality, *as this is what women tend to focus on.*

Many women love gray hair because it makes men look more mature and seductive. Often, women do not care about appearances at all if a man can make them laugh. Instead of trying to hide their insecurities, men should embrace them, and just accept that they are part of who they are *as a human.*

Men and Flirting

In the last section, we saw how men tend to have wrong notions about the perceptions women have about them. Men have certain desires and ideas that rarely get fulfilled because they aren't comfortable presenting their ideas. In this section, let us have a look at some of those ideas, which will help you understand the masculine psyche in a better way.

Drinks

Men love it when women offer to buy them drinks. They feel flattered and elated.

Hair

Men love it when women run their fingers through their hair; if combined with a seductive smile, men will love it! This is an intimate and sensual form of flirting. Do not overdo it, though, or it may seem too erotic or sexual.

Clarity

Men generally do not pick up on clues and cues properly. Therefore, many men often fail to acknowledge your presence or flirting, just because they have never been flirted with before. If you feel that the man you are flirting with is not interested in you or that he does not understand what you are doing, then try to be as clear as possible. In most cases, he probably does not know that you are flirting with him. Sometimes, it is better to forgo your coyness and simply flirt.

Smart

Nobody likes fake people, and men are no exception to this rule. Due to some unfortunate stereotypes perpetuated about men, many women think that men do not like women who are confident, bold, and smarter than them. Women think that men feel intimidated by such women. Therefore, many times women try to "dumb down," and while men don't mind bimbos, if you deliberately act like one, then they are sure to see through your game! Plus, it's impossible to continue this fakery for a long time.

Conversation

It is necessary to converse with your date properly. Men like women who can hold a decent conversation on any topic and provides a sign of good chemistry.

Makeup

While you should never apply makeup to please others, you can use the magic of beauty products to enhance your *already beautiful features*. Do not overdo it or underdo it if you are doing it for someone else. This does not mean that you should change your style, appearance, or attire for anyone. Stay true to yourself as much as possible.

Compliments

There is hardly anyone in this world who does not like receiving compliments. Men love them too, and they appreciate them more than anyone else because men hardly ever get compliments. Friends and strangers both avoid giving compliments to men. Men love it when women compliment them for a variety of things.

Subtleness

Women often believe that to appear flirty and "available," they need to act overtly sensual and sexual. This is false. Many men prefer subtlety as well. They would rather have women who flirt in a subtle way more than women who act overtly erotic.

Race/Bigotry

Men, especially men of color, hate it when Caucasian women or women other than those of their own race, fetishize them for the color of their skin. This is a shallow approach toward attraction, as it says nothing about their appearance and their personality. If you really want to compliment them for their skin, instead of talking about the color, consider commenting on smooth and beautiful it is. Exotification is a huge problem that needs to be addressed.

Eyes

Sometimes coquettishness is the way to go. To do this, just look into his eyes for a moment and then look away quickly. Almost all men find this attractive.

Self-Confidence

It pays to be yourself. Do not try to fake a personality just to impress a man. Men hate people who are fake. Instead of faking a personality, just try to develop your own personality. For instance, if you like reading, start reading more, if you like to dance, invest some time into it.

Dance

Another thing that many men love but are afraid to do is dance. Men love to dance, but they rarely do it on their own. If you are at a club, pull your man onto the dance floor and dance with him. This will help you create sweet memories as well.

Sense of Humor

Almost all men consider themselves funny, even if they are not. Humor them sometimes by laughing at their jokes, even if they aren't that funny! Laughing is a great way to appreciate the hard work that men put into being humorous. But do not laugh if you ever feel that the humor is crass or disgusting; bigotry should never be tolerated.

Be Yourself

Every individual is different. Try to maintain your individuality. Understand your true self and present it with confidence. If you are not confident with yourself, you will not be able to flirt confidently.

Smiling

Smiling is one of the easiest methods of flirting, but you need to understand how to do it correctly. Many women think that only smiling and doing nothing else is a simple and effective method of flirting that men understand. This is a myth. Men need much more than a smile to understand your intentions. For men, just smiling does not mean flirting.

Chapter Two: Understanding Flirting

Flirting is one of the most natural, yet one of the most complex, human behavioral concepts. It is a highly individualistic concept, which means that every person flirts in a different and singular way. There are many ways of flirting, which include various verbal, non-verbal, physical, and non-physical methods. But before moving on to these methods, it is necessary to understand the concept of flirting itself. In this chapter, let us put flirting under a microscope and try to understand what it is composed of.

Flirting

Flirting was once upon a time known as coquetry. Some people still use this word to define flirting, but the meaning of coquetry has changed slightly over the years. Flirting is often considered to be a form of sexual communication or behavior. While it is true that flirting is deep-set in sexuality and eroticism, discarding it as just a sexual behavior is a grave injustice to the concept. Flirting has developed into a much more complex and highly social behavior now, often accomplished with the help of written or spoken forms of communication. Flirting is also possible with the help of various non-verbal gestures and body movements. It is generally performed to attract a person.

In almost all the cultures around the world, society disapproves of rampant, explicit, and obvious displays of sexual excitement or advances socially. Similarly, such a display is also looked down upon in private settings if the persons are not romantically inclined towards each other. Indirect suggestions and advances often replace such direct displays. These indirect suggestions are a part of flirting.

Flirting generally involves behaving as well as talking in a certain manner that is suggestive. Your manner should suggest intimacy and boldness, albeit always within the rules of social manners and etiquette. This means a direct display of feelings should be avoided. This direct display should be replaced with irony, metaphors, sensual manner, wordplay, and general playfulness. Double entendre and puns are often used for flirting. Body language and bodily gestures such as open stances, hair flicking, eye contact, proximity, brief touches, and others are used as a form of flirting as well. There are many ways of flirting, as stated above, but generally, it is done in a shy, under-exaggerated, or frivolous style.

Verbal Flirting - Verbal Flirting Generally Includes Challenges

The flirter teases the other party by feigning disinterest, asking random questions, etc. This is done to increase (or add) tension to the situation. It helps the flirter to check the intention of the person and the amount of affection present in the situation. This section also includes things such as displaying poise, knowledge, approval, self-assurance, stylish nature, etc. A commanding attitude is another aspect that comes under this section.

Vocal

While flirting, the flirter changes his or her voice and modulates it. For instance, he or she may change the tone, intonation, volume, or pace of the voice. He or she may change all these together as well.

The concept of flirting and what is accepted as flirting varies according to nation and culture. This is due to the varied positions of social etiquette that change according to culture. These rules guide things such as proximity of people, the duration of eye contact, how much touching is permissible, the appropriateness of words, etc. Still, some behaviors are common throughout most cultures. For instance, smiling and head-tilting is a universal form of flirting.

How People Flirt

As said above, flirting is an essential aspect of social interaction. It is excessively common, yet, still difficult to understand. You may see it (or do it) every day, but understanding it is a different concept altogether. A lot of research has been conducted on flirting by psychologists and sociologists alike. In this section of this chapter, let us have a look at different styles of flirting, such as nonverbal and verbal behaviors.

The Five Styles

As per research, flirting can be divided into five major styles of flirting. These styles differ from person to person. Let us now have a brief look at all these styles.

Physical

The individuals who use this style generally flirt by showing physical behavior and using a lot of gestures. They feel comfortable physically and do so instead of using verbal communication cues. They find it easy to show their attraction with various physical cues. The behavior of such people is often considered to be sexual.

Sincere

People who use this style of flirting generally try to form an emotional connection with the opposite person. They try to form a bond with their romantic partner. This is why people who use this form of flirting generally cultivate intimacy early in the relationship. Such people often desire social support and provide it as well. This kind of flirting is generally romantic in nature. But this does not mean that it can't be sexual as well.

Playful

Individuals who use this style of flirting usually flirt in a lighthearted and playful manner as well. They don't care about how their behavior can be interpreted, but instead look at flirting from a satisfying point of view. They don't mind if their flirting does not end up turning into something serious.

Traditional

People who employ this kind of flirting generally tend to behave well. They like to stay in the boundaries of the stereotypical gender roles. This means that they generally allow men to initiate and women to reciprocate. They strictly follow traditional courtship rules. In this style, women generally take a passive role.

Polite

People who tend to have this kind of flirting style look at courtship from a cautious point of view. People may confuse these flirters for being too aggressive, inappropriate, or even needy.

Verbal and Nonverbal Flirting Behaviors

In this section, let us now have a look at the verbal and non-verbal styles of flirting. There are certain traditional roles that are associated with flirting. Here is a small list of these roles:

• Men generally take an active role in the process of courtship. Both men and women believe that a man should always initiate the courtship process.

• Women tend to take on a passive role in the process of courtship. They are receptive to signs, including verbal and nonverbal cues. They use eye contact a lot.

• Eye contact and signaling with eyes are generally used by women; however, both the genders tend to use these gestures a lot. Flirtatious eye contact is a common flirting technique. This is especially common in the beginning stages of courtship and interaction.

● Women generally smile a lot while talking to a person they like. This is generally observed in the later stages of the courtship and interaction.

In the initial stages of the approach, men tend to use various space-maximizing movements. This includes appearing as big as possible by adjusting and extending arms etc. Men also tend to reduce their closed-body positions. These positions include crossings legs, crossing arms, etc.

In the initial stages of interaction and courtship, both partners tend to pay compliments to each other a lot.

Implementing this Information

Understanding flirting techniques is essential. It can help you on these three fronts:

Improvement

You can improve your flirting style if you understand the intricacies of flirting carefully.

Situation

Understanding the nuances of a situation is essential for flirting. You should be able to adapt and change your style of flirting according to the need or time and situation. Similarly, you should also consider the person and his likes and dislikes as well.

Preselection

Understanding the different styles of flirting can also help you develop a smart process of preselection that will help you understand the process of courtship in a better way. It will help you make correct choices. It will also help you understand whether a person is worth knowing or not.

Improving Your Own Flirting Style

It is possible to make your own flirting style more unique and effective if you understand the intricacies of flirting. It can help you understand your weaknesses and work on them. Similarly, it can also help you understand your strengths and make them even stronger.

For instance, if you now realize that you generally use the physical style of flirting, you can utilize it effectively. For instance, you can select situations that require more physical interactions. These include clubbing, dancing, etc. You should generally avoid situations where physical intimacy is either not required or outright impossible- i.e., online.

If you generally use the polite style of flirting, you will notice that it is difficult for you to get your interest noticed by others. It is your natural attitude to act reserved, but if you ever want to display or convey your interest, you will have to change your flirting style slightly. You need to become somewhat forthcoming.

Tailoring Your Flirting

You can also change your flirting style according to your partner. This means that you can change your flirting style in such a way that it can help you understand your partner better. It also means changing and modifying your flirting style according to the flirting style of your partner.

For instance, if your partner loves a playful style of flirting, but you generally use the physical style of flirting, it is recommended to change the style of flirting and make it more playful. If your partner enjoys a more conservative style of flirting, you can adapt your personal style accordingly and make it more conservative.

Deciding Whom to Approach

Understanding the nuances of flirting styles can also help you to choose your future or potential partners. It can allow you to select partners in a much better way. For instance, you can match your flirting style to that of your partner and see whether your flirting style will complement their flirting style or not. If you feel that his flirting style is too different from yours, you may find the interaction difficult.

While the compatibility of flirting styles can really help you significantly, it does not mean that you and your potential boyfriend need to have the same flirting style. It means that you should instead try to adapt your flirting style and modify it to form a more homogenous interaction.

For instance, if you generally use a playful style of flirting, you will notice that this style does not work well with the conservative or polite style of flirting. But it can work well with the sincere style of the flirting and physical style of flirting as well!

While complimentary flirting style can help you with your interactions, it does not mean that you should focus on these styles only. Do not be apprehensive about approaching someone just because your flirting styles do not complement each other. In many cases, people with the opposite flirting styles have had long and successful relationships.

Reminder

While dealing with different styles of flirting, you should always remember that flirting is a highly individualized concept. The five different styles are present in varying amounts in all individuals. This means that a person can have a mixture of traditional flirting style with playful flirting style as well. Many times, people change their flirting style according to the situation. So instead of judging a person right away, try to analyze their personality carefully. This will help you avoid making rash decisions.

In the next chapter, we'll have a look at one of the most common types of flirting in modern times - Online Flirting.

Chapter Three: To Flirt or Not to Flirt Online

One of the greatest gifts of technology and modern times is the Internet. The Internet has made our lives extremely easy and simple. You can find anything and everything on the Internet now. This includes love, as well. In fact, many people find the Internet to be a much better (and quicker) place to find and meet new people as compared to the traditional methods.

According to many people, one of the biggest benefits of online dating is that you can use a variety of filters to nitpick through potential lovers. You can find people who like the same things or hate the same things quickly. Similarly, the Internet can also help you meet people with whom your paths would never cross in real life. But Internet dating and flirting are not all sweet and rosy. There are many cons of Internet dating as well. For instance, online dating can help you find quick dates, but is it really a great place to find someone special who will stay with you forever?

There still exists a stigma against Internet dating. While people do agree that there is a multitude of benefits associated with online dating, they would still rather prefer meeting someone offline. This is due to the regressive portrayal of Internet dating in the media.

Similarly, the overtly romanticized portrayal of traditional dating to have tarnished the image of online dating.

Internet Dating Tips

In this section, let us have a look at some simple Internet or online dating tips that will help you avoid heartbreak and betrayal.

Do Your Research

Before beginning to use online platforms, it is recommended to conduct thorough research. There are many different dating sites and apps available online that offer users a plethora of choices, algorithms, and options as well. Some sites and apps are generic that come with many filters to help you choose men according to your taste. There are some niche dating apps and sites, as well. These can be related to anything, for instance, religion, pets, education, age group, etc. While many people think that online dating is much easier than regular dating, it is not. The only thing easy about online dating is meeting people. Otherwise, like traditional dating, it is also a concept that is based on the trial and error method.

Fewer Photos, More Details

People have become obsessed with posting pictures of their daily lives online. Many people tend to add as many pictures as possible on their dating profiles. Researchers believe that this is a bad strategy if you are trying to attract serious people. Your dating profile should not contain more than five photos. These photos should be curated carefully. They should be able to represent who you are and what your beliefs are. Try to select images that are positive or show your positive side. Showing your negative sides on dating profiles is much worse than showing it offline.

The photos that you choose to upload online should show your true emotions and feelings. It is necessary to pair your pictures with a simple description of yourself. Instead of going for a generic and commonsensical style of expressing yourself, you should try to include something that will prove that you are a unique individual. It should make your profile stand out among the thousands of profiles. Do not expect to get a lot of matches if your profile is generic.

Your profile should hold enough mystery while giving away crucial insights about you. The more truthful you are, the better the chances of meeting interesting people will be. While your insightful profile does not guarantee long-term compatibility, it does mean that you will be able to go on interesting dates. Similarly, it will also ensure that you are going out with a man who shares your likes and dislikes. It will also help you prepare yourself well.

Watch Out for the Lies and the Liars

One of the biggest problems associated with online dating is that people tend to lie a lot while being online. Deception is a rampant problem that plagues online dating. It is easy to fool someone online. A lot of people generally create their own dating profiles, but nowadays, some people also pay people to create dating profiles for them. These professionals are experts in creating dating profiles, which attract people easily. These profiles tend to create a false image of the person.

Catfishing is not a rare problem anymore, but still, your falling into the trap of catfishing attempts is less likely. But this does not mean that you are safe from deception. Many people tend to tell small lies that they think are harmless just to attract dates. The deception is quite gendered as well. For instance, men generally lie about their height or their salary (and almost always about the size of their penis). Women tend to lie about their age. It's clear that these deceptions are based on the stereotypes that are associated with each gender.

Problems

While it is true that online dating has revolutionized the world of dating forever, it has also created a multitude of problems as well. For instance, problems such as "ghosting" and "orbiting" have given rise to stalker-like behavior. Passive stalking is a curse associated with online dating. While passive stalking was always present, online dating has made it easy and more accessible. Before Instagram and

Facebook, people still used to creep up on others, but now thanks to social media, this process has become easier and safer.

There are many problems associated with online dating. But this does not mean that online dating cannot help you in many aspects as well. It still is a great way to meet new people. It is a great way to expand your horizons and dating pool as well. But you need to vigilant and constantly aware of the things that happen online.

In the next section, let us have a look at the different Pros and Cons of Online Dating.

Pros and Cons of Online Dating

Online dating is a complex experience. It involves a lot of things – both good and bad. For instance, there are many people who have met their soulmate online. But there are also many women who only receive two things from online dating apps: disappointment and unsolicited pictures of the man's penis. In this section, let us have a look at some of the common pros and cons of online dating.

Let us first have a look at the pros of online dating.

Singles Everywhere

Unlike real life dating where you need to check whether a man is single or not, in online dating, you can be more assured that a man is single. This means you do need to play a guessing game. Similarly, you do not need to guess a man's sexuality; it should be obvious if he is looking for a female mate!

Number

There are a lot of people looking for love online. This means that you will never face a dearth of singles around you.

Ideas

One of the biggest pros of online dating is that you can check out certain details about the man you plan to go on a date with beforehand. This will help you know which topics to broach and which to avoid.

Comfort

Online dating can be done from anywhere- the looking part, i.e., you do not need to go out to find someone and court them.

Expenses

Going out frequently to find potential dates is an expensive affair. Similarly, if you approach matchmakers to find a date for you, you will face a lot of additional expenses as well. Compared to these options, online dating is cost-effective. There are many apps and websites that offer their services for free. The apps that do not offer their services for free offer them quite cheaply. This makes online dating a highly affordable deal.

People

Online dating expands your dating pool to infinity. You can meet some of the most interesting people and get some offbeat stories, as well. Even if you do not end dating, you can always meet new and interesting friends using these apps.

Mate

You may even find your soulmate online (if you search properly) because you will be able to check out and understand everything about your potential date, discarding the ones that do not match your tastes.

Let's have a look at the cons of online dating.

Creeps

You can never guess whether a person is genuine and "good" until you meet them. Online dating sites are full of creepy men, and you can enter dangerous territory quickly. It is difficult to avoid such bizarre personalities online.

Time

Online dating takes a lot of time. You need to weed out a lot of people by checking out their details one by one. It can cause a lot of eyestrain as well.

Online dating can also be quite overwhelming because of the implications associated with it. It is a troublesome experience to reject people based on superficial characteristics.

Rejection

People get rejected all the time, but these rejections are worse online. *Everyone gets rejected online,* but what makes online rejections worse is the fact that they are often superficial. People can reject you based on the vaguest things, including the color of your eyes.

Choice

According to the paradox of choice, the more options we get, the sadder we become because we get befuddled due to the sheer number of choices. The grass is always greener on the other side. This makes your dating life unstable, and you end up going on first dates almost every other day.

Clueless People

Online dating is quite different from real-life dating, and the tactics and techniques that are used in real life are rarely successful in online dating. For instance, women love mysterious men in real life, but they abhor blank profiles online. Blank profiles, incorrect or unflattering photos, lack of details, etc. are some of the most common reasons why online dating can be a nuisance.

Randos

Online dating expands your horizons of dating and allows you to meet people you would never have met in real life. Unfortunately, it does so for everyone, which means that you often get contacted by random men. It is impossible to avoid such people online. These men often try to harass or gaslight women into dating them. While there are options to block or report such profiles online, it does not work all the time. For instance, if you block a creepy man's profile once, he may create another one - just to harass you.

Falsifications

This is one of the biggest problems associated with online dating. Everything is not what it seems in the world of online dating. A person's profile may look great, his pictures may look dazzling, but when he shows up for the real date, all your expectations may shatter immediately. People often lie about themselves online. They act coy and perfect online, but in real life, their real face – and personality – appears.

No Body Language

One of the biggest problems with online dating is that you cannot use body language and gestures. It becomes impossible to judge and understand people properly if you cannot see how they behave and act around other people. Eyes are windows to the soul. In online dating, you cannot see their eyes. Similarly, a lot of deception can happen in online dating.

Online dating is especially difficult for flirting, as you need to depend on texts and voice to do it. Modern flirting uses a lot of gestures and body language to convey non-verbal messages.

It is, therefore, clear that online dating is a complex topic. While it has its benefits, it has a lot of cons as well. It is especially difficult to flirt online. Therefore, it is up to the discretion of the reader, whether to date online or not.

Chapter Four: Appearance: Does it Really Count?

According to many women, a desirable man needs to be kind, intelligent, understanding, family-oriented, etc. Most of these women also believe that men should have a sense of humor and should look decent. But the question is which one of these is the most attractive of all the other traits. According to various research, it has been proven that many people rank every other trait higher than good looks. But this is not reflected in real life generally. In fact, many people tend to focus on good looks more than anything else. While other traits may come into play later, people generally tend to select their mates by looking at their appearance and outer looks first. Everything else comes later. The initial attraction must happen, and that is based on looks whether we like it or not.

Even in online dating, we stop at profiles where the man in the pictures looks charming and attractive. This proves that we do consider good looks or physical appearance to be attractive. In this chapter, let us have a look at this phenomenon in detail.

Physical Attractiveness is More Important Than We Think

Physical appearance and attractiveness are like the gatekeeper to other aspects of a mate. Physical appearance shows that your potential mate is of age, looks healthy, and can reproduce as well. Therefore, physical appearance automatically dominates our mind while choosing a mate. It is pure evolutionary biology. We tend to pursue a relationship with a person who we find attractive. This attraction can be of any kind, but generally, it starts with physical attraction.

Men - both gay and straight - are more inclined to physical attractiveness than women. They understand how important it is. Still, according to research conducted on online dating sites, it was found that both men and women pay close attention to their physical looks and attractiveness. Both care about their general appearance. With this, attractiveness also forms an important part of all our dating decisions. We consider attractiveness more important than intelligence, personality, and education.

According to researchers, physical attractiveness is important to us because we tend to attach certain positive qualities with it. For instance, we tend to believe that the people who are physically attractive are often happier and more pleasant than the individuals who are not physically attractive. Similarly, it was observed that these kinds of associations are present in almost all cultures. The notions of physical attractiveness may change according to culture, but what this attractiveness stands for remains constant. For instance, once upon a time, extreme paleness was highly attractive in Europe, but now it is all about dark skin. Yet, the notions associated with both these factors, i.e., attractiveness equals happiness (and others), remain the same.

There has been a lot of research to counter the research above. In the next section, let us have a look at this research and its results, giving you the full picture.

Physical Attractiveness is Less Important than We Think

According to research, one of the main reasons why we fail to consider the importance of physical attraction is because we do not want partners who are extremely attractive physically. We are satisfied with partners who are just "regularly" attractive. According to research, moderately attractive as well as attractive partners are better than partners who are not attractive at all. Similarly, if a person is less attractive, then he or she is associated with negative qualities. But positive qualities do not require a lot of attractiveness either. If a person is moderately attractive, he or she is associated with positive qualities. This proves that people can find moderately attractive people acceptable and can accept them as a potential mate as well. This might seem to be complicated and convoluted, but to understand this properly, you just need to have a look at the difference between needs and greed.

The difference between needs and greed can help you understand the paradox of moderate levels of physical attraction effectively. A need is something that you like a lot, but if it is available in high amounts, you tend to care less for it. Greed or luxury are not important when the needs are not met. But once the basic needs are met, luxury or greed becomes highly desirable. According to this theory, everyone looks at moderate attractiveness as a need, while anything more than that is a luxury. When people say that physical attractiveness is not important to them, they are most probably always referring to "greed" or a "luxury" level of attractiveness. This means, when people say that they do not care (or do not desire) physical attractiveness, they are talking about the exceptional levels of attractiveness. Of course, they want a person who is moderately attractive, though.

What Exactly is Moderately Attractive?

The concept of moderately attractive is subjective and changes from individual to individual. Everyone agrees that supermodels are incredibly attractive, but everyone disagrees with the definition of moderately attractive. Most attractive people generally have a narrow range of "attractiveness" while people who are less attractive generally have a larger range of "unattractiveness." This means people who are less attractive will consider a lot of people attractive to moderately attractive.

If you and your partner are on the same levels of physical attractiveness, your relationship will most likely last longer. But this is not the only thing that will make your relationship last. There are multiple things to consider if you want to make your relationship last for a long time. Relationships are built on trust and mutual respect. If these two factors are not present in your relationship, no amount of physical attractiveness can salvage it.

Therefore, while physical attractiveness is important, it is not the most important thing in the world. Even if you are not attractive, you will always find a beau who will love you and cherish you forever.

Chapter Five: Confidence - Why It Matters and How to Boost It

No one is born with confidence. It is an acquired trait that people learn over time. No one is fully confident all the time. The levels of confidence fluctuate according to the situation, place, person, and time. Just talking about it will never help you get it. Self-confidence is an essential trait that everyone needs to have. But it is also quite challenging to acquire because of societal pressures. Women find it particularly difficult to develop self-confidence because girls are taught to be shy and coy during their upbringing. Women are taught to be caregivers from birth, which is why we tend to think of others before ourselves. We tend to put the needs of others before our own needs. Therefore, we do not spend a lot of time developing ourselves. Girls are often encouraged to be less daring, to be passive, and less bold. This is done so that we do not become threats to the men around us. But these old practices need to be buried now.

Turn on the television and see how women have changed and how they are becoming more and more self-confident. There are thousands of examples of confident women around you who have changed their world, just based on their self-confidence. These women possess the chutzpah that many other women do not have.

But really, do these women possess something special that others do not? The answer to this question is obviously no. Every woman, or for that matter, every person born in this world has a certain level of chutzpah. This chutzpah remains untouched and is unused. You need to tap into it often to remind yourself of the courage and bravery that you possess.

Self-confidence is essential in every field of life. You cannot do anything successfully if you are not self-confident. Self-confidence is necessary while flirting as well. To flirt with a man requires a lot of strength and confidence. Therefore, many women are afraid of approaching men because they fear facing humiliation and public failure. But this does not mean that you cannot develop self-confidence. Let us now have a look at some tips that can help you become self-confident and bold.

Responsibility

If you want to be self-confident, you need to learn how to take responsibility for yourself. You cannot be self-confident unless you are responsible for yourself. If you wait for things to happen on their own or if you think that Lady Luck will shower her fortunes on you, then you will never succeed in life. Waiting for the guy to hit on, you will take forever. Sometimes it is better to take risks and take things into your own hands. Self-confidence is not magic. No amount of prayers will help you become self-confident. It is a path full of difficulties that you must tread. This path needs to be trodden alone, as well. So, it is time to take matters into your hands and become responsible for your own destiny.

Experiments

These experiments are not related to science. To become self-confident, you need to start experimenting with your life. For instance, if you feel awkward around people, go out and have dinner alone. Join a dance class. Teach yourself new things, such as learning a musical instrument. Test your abilities. Talk to people. See that your abilities are opening new horizons to you.

Action Plan

Every great thing has started with a plan. You cannot achieve success if you do not plan for it. It is recommended to choose a topic and work on it until you develop it thoroughly. These topics can include professional or personal development, as well. It is recommended to develop an action plan and formulate the steps that will take you toward your goal. Making excuses won't cut it. Every tiny step that you take will ultimately take you toward your goal. Every small step will boost your confidence, as well.

Stick to the Plan

Just making the plan is not important; you need to stick to it as well. When you take a new challenge, it is necessary to stick to it as best you can. Self-confidence is not automatic. You need to work hard for it. Each attempt is important, but don't worry if you fail at any point. Just pick yourself up and start working again. Whether you succeed in the long term or not solely depends on how dedicated and passionate you are. Follow through your plan until you taste the sweet taste of success. Do not rest until then.

Act "As If"

Do not wait for the plan to finish to become confident. Confidence is all about faking until you make it. This means that even if you are not confident about something, you just need to work hard and act like you are confident all the time. This is a common psychological trick. You can change your behavior if you believe hard enough. You can change your feelings, your emotions, and your confidence level as well. You just need to believe in yourself and act like you are extremely confident all the time. Once you start faking confidence on the outside, the true, inside confidence will follow soon as well.

Mentor

If you feel that you are not confident and cannot do it on your own, don't worry. You can use the help of a mentor. A mentor is any person related to your field (or not) who is highly dedicated, motivated, and confident. You are supposed to observe them and see how they live their life. For instance, if you are trying to become self-confident about your looks or flirting with men, talk to a woman who is an expert at both things. Observe this woman and learn how she tackles her day-to-day life. Meet the woman and tell her about your problem. Tell her how you plan to solve it. In most cases, this woman will be more than willing to help you. Get her feedback about your action plan. Remember, it is all about faking it until you make it.

Therefore, confidence is something that can be cultivated with ample dedication and practice. It is not difficult to become a person who is confident. You just need to formulate an action plan and work on it meticulously. So do not wait any more, just step up and start working on your confidence right away.

Chapter Six: Play It Like Cleopatra! 3 Ancient Secrets to Attracting Men

Cleopatra is one of the most iconic women in the world. She singlehandedly changed the destiny of the world with the help of her charms, wit, and the power of seduction. Cleopatra is often considered to be one of the top ten queens to ever rule the world.

Cleopatra was the last Pharaoh of Egypt. She was well known for being a legendary seductress. The legends of her seductive powers are still repeated all the time. Every woman can learn from Cleopatra. But before moving on to the things that you can learn from her, it is necessary to have a brief look at her life.

Cleopatra was born in 69 BC. Her father was Ptolemy XII "Auletes," who was a Pharaoh as well. She was the last Pharaoh of Egypt because, during her reign, Rome was ready to take over her kingdom. Cleopatra started her reign side by side with her brother Ptolemy, but this arrangement did not last for too long.

Cleopatra's name has been associated with two men - Mark Antony and Julius Caesar. Both these men were incredibly powerful and strong. She fell in love with Mark Antony after Caesar was brutally murdered by his friends Brutus and Cassius. Many years passed after this, and she finally committed suicide because she lost a battle against a Roman called Octavian.

Her story has been used for various literary endeavors, the most famous being by Shakespeare. After Shakespeare, the person who made her extremely famous was Elizabeth Taylor when she acted in a movie based on her life in 1963.

Cleopatra was one of the most beautiful temptresses to ever walk the earth. She was bold, beautiful, and smart. But not all people agree that Cleopatra was beautiful. Some believe that she was more intelligent and shrewder than beautiful. There are many myths associated with the life of Cleopatra, which has made her life quite controversial. No one can say for sure whether she was beautiful or not.

But it does not matter whether Cleopatra was beautiful or not. What matters more is that she used her feminine charms and the power of seduction to seduce her way through difficulties. She wielded a lot of power, especially in a time when women were inferior to men. She was supposed to be extremely intelligent. She had a great voice and was knowledgeable about a lot of things. She was especially attractive and could subjugate anyone with her charms and wits. Even a dying man would become attracted to her charms.

Let us now have a look at the three things that every woman can learn from Cleopatra:

Tip 1

Look after yourself and care for yourself as well. Do not spend a lot of time grooming yourself. Instead, try to focus on your self-confidence and self-esteem. Nothing is sexier than a person who is bold and confident. Practice how to display your intelligence. It is also recommended to learn a few things about politics, power, and the potency of attraction. You need to understand the intricacies of life if you ever want to succeed. A woman who is bold and has a lot of confidence can take life by its horns and defeat it at its own game. Cleopatra was confident enough to seduce the most powerful man in the world. She not only seduced Julius Caesar but also bore him a son. She was able to do this based on her knowledge, her flirting skills, and, most important of all, her confidence. Without confidence, Cleopatra would have failed miserably and would have died at the hands of her brother.

Tip 2

Don't follow the rules to the T. Rules are meant to be broken, especially if they restrict you unjustly. You need to cultivate a sense of self-confidence. You need to find a new "self" that will be bolder, more confident, more stylish, and especially strong. Certain rules should be broken. Remember, flirting is supposed to be organic. You are trying to win over a man and not a machine. Instead of following all the rules carefully, break a few. If breaking the rules can help you get your man, then break them away.

For instance, the rules say that you must wait for the man to initiate the courtship. But if you believe that you can expedite the process, initiate the process of courtship yourself. Ultimately, it is all about getting your man to like you and make him attracted to you. All is well that ends well.

Tip 3

Always aim high. You need to put in a lot of energy into everything that you undertake. Never half-ass things. It is always better to put in your whole energy. Only serious efforts will lead you to success. Looks matter, but what matters more than looks is your confidence, your integrity, and your intellect. A generic looking smart person will always be more successful than a beautiful but dumb person.

Ultimately, Cleopatra has now become synonymous with beauty, but she was surely much more than that. If you want to mimic her, try to emulate her style, confidence, and intellect instead of focusing on her physical attributes. Her intellect will help you become a great flirter/ seductress.

Chapter Seven: Signs of High-Value Men (and Where to Find Them)

Many times, women are scared to approach men because they do not know whether the man they are interested in is worth approaching or not. Women love to date men who are "high value." They despise men who are ignorant, irritating, and crass. But understanding whether a man is high value or not can be quite complex. In this section, let us have a look at 20 things that all high-value men possess. If you find a man who possesses these qualities, then rest assured; he is a high-value man and a keeper as well.

He Commits to Himself and Others

A high-value man is committed to his life and his life goals. He will always work hard to make his life better. He will also work hard to make the life of his friends and girlfriend better. He considers his family, career, and life important. He knows what he can offer and will only approach a woman if he thinks she will be interested in him. He is not interested in anything vague. He likes being committed and will not falter at the sign of emotions.

He Makes an Effort

He puts a lot of effort into all the things that he does. This includes his wardrobe, his attire, his overall look, etc. He also pays close attention to what his woman wants. He never wants to fall short in front of his women. He is a master of detail. He likes everything done in a meticulous and bold manner. He will never ask a woman about what she wants to do because he knows what she likes and what she does not like. He knows how to please her. You will always feel safe and comfortable with a high-value man. He also puts in an effort in the bedroom as well. A high-value man is never satisfied unless his woman is satisfied. He wants to please his woman as much as he can. For him, the pleasure of his woman is the most important thing in the world.

He Makes Plans and Follows Through

A high-value man is good at making plans. He knows the value of time and will always have a busy schedule full of action and activity. He balances his personal as well as professional life properly. If he makes a plan, he will surely follow it through. So, if he plans a date with you, rest assured that he will make all the arrangements on time. If the date involves some form of activity, such as hiking or dancing, he will ask his date to pack her bag to fit the event. He likes to surprise his woman, but he does not want her to get caught out in an awkward situation.

He is a Great Conversationalist

A high-value man knows how to talk. He reads, he watches movies, he watches plays, and he attends seminars as well. He is a polymath and knows a lot of things, but he does not show it off all the time. He does not like to brag. His life is full of interesting experiences, and he has many stories to tell. He is open and is not scared to answer questions about himself. He displays an interest in his woman's life by asking are pertinent and relevant questions as well. He does not just care about her outer looks, for a high-value man, the insides count as well.

He Dresses and Grooms Himself Impeccably

A high-value man knows how to dress well and look dapper. This does not mean that he spends a lot of money on his clothes and attire. A person can look good and stylish without spending a lot of money. He spends time to care for himself. He understands style. He knows how to recreate the top designer looks for a fraction of the price. He would rather buy a large jacket and then tailor it to fit him properly. He goes to the gym and is fit. His shoes are always impeccable. He cuts his nails properly. He knows his colognes and wears them in the proper amount. He never overdoes anything. His hair is trimmed. His unwanted hair is either plucked or shaved or trimmed. This includes ear hairs, rogue eyebrow hairs, and nose hair as well. He understands that caring for yourself is a universal trait that members of all the genders must follow.

He Understands a Woman of Value

He understands that he cannot get everything he desires. He does not whine about rejection. He also does not start commenting about the woman who rejected him. He understands that attraction is a personal thing, and it is subjective to a lot of factors. He does not mind if a woman does not choose him. He will not give her a hard time just because she did not choose him. He will just wish her good luck and go on his way instead.

His Car and Home are Clean

A high-value man hates trash and junk. He believes that staying clean is an essential habit. He likes to keep his car and his house clean. He likes to maintain order in his home. Everything in his house is clean. His bed is always made, his toilets are clean and fresh, his yard is never cluttered. He is meticulous about keeping things clean and tidy.

He's Fun!

A high-value man is aware that he is a funny and humorous person. A high-value man works hard, but he also plays hard. If someone is playing music and if the occasion is appropriate, he will surely dance. If there is a karaoke machine, he will be the first one to sing. He is a man who likes to live his life fully. Even if he is introverted, he will still have a lot of fun. He will also help others to have a lot of fun as well.

He's Clear On His Intentions

A high-value man is always clear with his intentions. You will never feel confused about him. He knows what he wants. He also knows what he can offer. He is there to offer you true love, if you are ready to reciprocate it. If he wants a committed relationship, he wants it to be perfect. A high-value man will always try to find a high-value woman, as well. He wants a woman who will not only encourage him but will inspire him as well. He wants a woman who adds to his life in a meaningful way. He wants a life partner who will help him follow his passions and dreams.

He Communicates Clearly

If a high-value man wants something, he will let you know it is a clear and efficient manner. If he does not like something about you, he will broach the subject in a diplomatic and professional way. He will never be crass or rude about anything. His goal is to reach an agreement and not to defeat others. If he ever feels that you are not ready to listen or hear his ideas, he will rather walk away than continue to talk to you.

He's Well Mannered

This is a given. A high-value man will always be well mannered. He will know how to eat at a fine dining restaurant. He will know what to do with a napkin while eating. He will always open the door for you and will offer you his hand. He will always put his hand on your back while leading you into a room. He will always hold your hand and carry it gracefully. If he must leave the table for a moment, he will get up and kiss you lightly. He never treats the wait staff, the valet, or the chauffeur rudely. For him, everyone is a human being who deserves respect and kindness.

He Shows the Right Amount of PDA

He knows when and how to show affection in public. He will never be crass about his display of affection.

He Seeks to Understand Women

A high-value man knows that no one is perfect in this world. He knows that people go through a lot of things in their day-to-day lives. A high-value man will always encourage a woman. He will help her rise, understand her heartbreak, and will always help her in all the walks of her life. He will help her follow her dreams. He will help her face her fears. He will help her accomplish things that she is capable of.

He understands and appreciates the beauty in chaos. He understands that life is not a piece of cake for everyone. Whenever he feels that his woman is feeling nervous or is sabotaging herself, he will help her see the light. He will help his woman to overcome her vulnerability and will help her grow as well. A high-value man knows that emotional bonding is far more crucial than physical bonding; he realizes that emotions are more important than sex or physical pleasure.

Therefore, it is clear that a high-value man is decent and bold. He is also charming and confident. Along with the above-mentioned qualities, there are many other qualities that a high-value man has. If a man possesses most of the qualities mentioned here, he is surely a high-value man; you should not let him get away!

Chapter Eight: The 21 Steps of Flirting

Flirting with a guy seems like an impossible task for many women because they find cute and hot men intimidating. Many women also have a constant fear of rejection, which they cannot ignore. But this does not mean that you should not try it! Flirting does not have to involve verbal actions; you can also flirt using a variety of gestures, expressions, and body language. Using these actions, you can even flirt across the room. A simple yet seductive smile, a bold hair flip, and an erotic look - all these are different ways of flirting with a man without using words. In-person you can flirt using various techniques as well. For instance, playful teasing, light touches, honest compliments are all different types of flirting techniques. You can even flirt using text messages. In this chapter, let us have a look at different types of flirting and how to use them.

For the convenience of the reader, this chapter has been divided into three sections:

Flirting From Across the Room

Let us first begin with the easiest types of all the three types of flirting: flirting from across the room.

Eye Contact

The importance of eye contact has been mentioned a few times in other chapters already. Eye contact is a great flirting technique that can be used at any time or any place. Eye contact is easy to do. You just need to do it in a limited amount, though. If you overdo it, you will end up looking like a creepy person who is obsessed with the man. Lingering eye contact is a great way to show that you are interested in someone. Eye contact is also a great test to check whether a man is interested in you or not. If you make eye contact with the guy and he holds eye contact, there are high chances that he is into you as well. But don't worry if he looks away, it is possible that he is shy and does not want to meet your eyes.

Another trick to check whether a guy is interested in you or not or when you want to display your interest is to look at the guy until he looks at you. Once he looks, just smile for a moment and look away. If you are feeling bold and cheeky, you can even throw in a wink to let your attraction be known.

Smiling

Another really simple way to display your interest is by smiling. According to many studies, smiling makes people seem more attractive. If you have beautiful teeth, flaunt them without any care.

Smiling makes people seem friendlier and happier as well. Smiling will make you look more approachable. If someone has a crush on you and he sees you smiling, he is more likely to come and greet you. If you act too grumpy, he will likely steer clear of you. Smiling also makes you feel happier. Happiness and confidence are the two keys to flirting. If you can flirt with confidence and a big smile on your face, you will seem attractive, and you will feel attractive as well.

Body Language

This is obvious; flirting requires the use of a lot of body moments and gestures. You cannot flirt properly without using body language. In fact, the flirting done with the help of bodily gestures is much more potent than that done with words. You don't even have to open your mouth to attract people and flirt with them. We have already covered two essential parts of body language for flirting, eye contact, and smiling, but there are other things that you should keep in mind as well.

Crossing Arms

Never cross your arms if you want to flirt with someone. Crossing arms is like the opposite activity to smiling. Smiling makes you seem happy, fun, and approachable while crossing your arms makes you seem like you are frustrated, angry, or cross. It will also scare him off because it makes you seem closed off and unapproachable. Some women (and men) tend to cross their arms when they are nervous. If you have the habit of doing this, pay close attention to it.

Flip Your Hair

Men love it when women flip her hair. Flipping hair is considered to be a very feminine and seductive action. It draws attention to your beautiful neck and to your long and pretty hair as well. It is also one of the best-known flirting techniques. So, if you want to flirt with a guy, just flip your hair in front of him- but don't be too obvious about it. There are other methods that you can use - for instance, playing with your hair is also a way to flirt with men.

Playing with Jewelry

Another common way to flirt with a man is to play with your jewelry. For instance, you can play with your necklace or pendant. This will draw his attention to your neckline. Men love the female neckline.

Get In His Way

Another really great way to flirt with a guy is to get in his path frequently. This does not mean that you should follow him or trouble him all the time. You just need to make some conscious effort to get into his path in a casual and nonchalant way. It should feel like destiny keeps on putting both of you around each other all the time. Do not be too obvious about this, or he will become suspicious.

If you work in the same office, walk around his desk a few times a day. If you both have dogs, take your dog to the same park where he walks his dog, etc. But don't overdo this. You don't want the guy to think that you are a stalker.

Look Your Best

This is quite obvious, but still, it needs to be said. Looking your best is essential if you want to feel confident and bold. It is necessary to look your best whenever your crush is around you. Looking your best does not mean that you should go around looking like a sleazy woman. Similarly, it does not mean going around in evening gowns all the time. You just need to dress carefully in clean and proper clothes. You just need to be well-groomed and dressed in a neat manner. If you look at your best, you will feel your best. If you feel confident about your looks, you will feel confident about flirting as well.

Here are some tips that can help you look your best:

● Keep your hair washed and clean regularly. It should always feel smooth and smell fresh.

● Brush your teeth. Your teeth do not need to be "fake" white.

● Shave around parts you find unfeminine.

● Make yourself pretty. This step includes a lot of things. For instance, if you like painting your nails, paint them. If you like wearing a lot of jewelry, wear it, etc.

● Wear clean clothes. Avoid dressing like a slob. Your clothes should be comfortable.

● Try different hairstyles. It should look like you put in some effort in your everyday look. You can also try out different hair colors. But don't overdo this, or it will do a lot of damage to your hair.

First Move

Traditionally men are supposed to make the first move, and it is recommended to wait if you can for him to take the initiative. But if you feel that it is becoming too much and that you cannot wait, it is time to take things into your own hands. Waiting for men to begin the pursuit is a boring and cumbersome task. If you get fed up with it, it is time to approach him on your own.

Flirting in Person

Talking

While body language is a great way to flirt with men, using your verbal prowess can help you get ahead of everyone. It can allow you to flirt in a far more open and involved way. Talking to your crush can help you tell him about a lot of things and express a lot of ideas that cannot be expressed using your body language. Talking to a crush is easy if you know what to talk about. If you don't, then some common topics on which you can talk about include recent events, school, work, etc.

Another great way to open a conversation is with the help of a question. Open your conversation with a question he will be forced to answer. Asking a question also shows that you are interested in a person and are not just interested in talking to yourself. You can ask him about some recent events, the latest books, the latest movies, etc. You can also ask him about what he did over the weekend.

It is recommended to avoid asking questions that can be answered in one word. For instance, do not ask him questions such as "Do you like this actor?" or "Is this your favorite book?" etc. If you ask such questions, then the conversation will surely die out as these are simple yes or no questions.

Another tip to get him talking is switching the conversation. Who does not love talking about themselves? Try to talk to him about things that he seems to be passionate about. These subjects will surely get him talking. For instance, if he loves sports, you can talk to him about sports as well.

Tip: While talking, it is recommended to use his name a lot. People love to hear their names being used by others, especially in a conversation, and especially when the opposite sex uses it. Calling your crush by his name is a great way to make him interested in you. It will also help you to create a sense of intimacy and affection.

Smile and Laugh

While we have already covered smiling, this kind of smiling is different. Smiling and laughing while you are talking to a person is different from smiling from a distance. Smiling throughout the conversation is important, as it will help you let your beau know that you like him and that you feel comfortable around him. He should understand that you like what he is saying that you enjoy his voice. Laughing and smiling frequently will also make you look attractive. It will make you seem like a fun-loving, happy, and cheerful person.

Laughing at a man's jokes is a great way to make him feel confident and bold. Men love to be funny, and they appreciate it when members of the opposite sex laugh at their jokes. If you do not like his jokes, just give a genuine courtesy laugh. Remember, do not cackle like a hag, or he will be scared out of his wits.

Touching

Communication is not just verbal. To enhance the intensity of verbal communication, it is necessary to get physical as well. Find ways in which you can touch your crush from time to time. This touch does not need to be too physical. A simple brush of fingers or a graze of the arm is enough. Touching your crush frequently is a great way to let your crush know that you are flirting with him. It will show him that you are willing to get physical. Here are some tips that can help you with this step:

Touch His Forearm Gently When You Are Talking

When he cracks a joke that you find funny, reach out and touch his arm while laughing. You can also do this while consoling him. Put your elbow or arm on his casually. This will create a feeling of camaraderie between the both of you. It will also prove that you feel comfortable around him. While walking together, lean into him "accidentally." If you are flirty enough, brush your hand against his hand and wait for his reaction.

Another way to flirt with a man is by straightening his collar. To do this, just tell him that his collar is crooked and fix it for him. You can do this without telling him. Just stand in front of him, look into his eyes, and straighten his collar gently. While doing this, brush your fingers gently across his neck. Once done, just look into his eyes and say, "Hmm, now that looks better" and gently back away.

Your Body

Men are visual beings. They understand things better when they are shown. They love when they get sneak peeks of your body here and there. This is a great way to let him know that you are attracted to him. To do this, just subtly draw his attention to your body from time to time. This will get his heart racing. It will also force him to conclude that he is interested in you. Below are some tricks that can help you.

One of the easiest ways to display your body is to ask the man whether you should get a belly button piercing. To do this, just pull up your top slightly and show him your belly button. Ask him whether it would look good or not. If he starts to stammer, well done, you have successfully caught his attention.

Pretend that you have some shoulder pain and that you would like a massage. Pull down your neckline slightly to show your skin. If you are lucky, he will give you a simple massage.

Lips work great for seduction and flirting. Lick your lips from time to time. This will make him think about kissing. You can also bite them, lick them, or apply some lipstick to draw his attention toward your lips. Do remember to be subtle while doing this!

It is recommended to do this in a limited way. Do not overdo it and always use these techniques in moderation. If you overdo them, he will think that you are desperate. If you are not on a beach, don't show up in a bikini. Remember, you want to attract a high-value man - not a sleazebag.

Dance

Dancing is one of the primal forms of attracting a mate. Dancing with him is a fun way to let your guy know that you like him. Dancing does not need to be too serious. You can dance anywhere; it does not matter. The only thing that matters is that you get some quality, one-on-one time with him.

It is recommended to make it obvious that you plan to choose him to dance with. Pull his hand and take him away from his group of friends. If he lets you take him away, then rest assured, he likes you as well. Sexy dancing is fine too! But do not overdo it. Do not be overtly sexual, and do not do dance styles such as grinding. It will make him uncomfortable, especially if there are people around him.

If your guy does know how to dance or is an awkward (or an outright bad) dancer, then it is your duty to make him feel comfortable. You can do this by slowly easing him into the dance, or you can join him by making some wacky moves as well. Just be sure that he does not feel mocked. If you can make him laugh, he will surely enjoy your company.

It is recommended to ease him into slow dancing as well. Slow dancing is sexy, seductive, and full of passion and romance. Look into his eyes while you are dancing. It will melt him like a chocolate bar.

Pay Him a Compliment

Many women think that only men are supposed to pay compliments. But this is a myth. Guys appreciate compliments too. In fact, everyone likes getting compliments. Appreciating your crush is a great way to show him that you like him. He will appreciate the interest that you are showing in him. He will also think that you are paying attention to him. If you do not know how to compliment men, check out the list, below, of things you can try!

Be Specific

Compliments need to be specific and personal. Generic compliments such as "You look great," "You look hot," "You are cute," are nice, but they are common. They are generic. He must have heard them before. He won't remember them. To make your compliment count, it is recommended to compliment him about something specific, like a specific trait or quirk. The compliment needs to be fresh. He will surely remember your compliment. One great way to make your compliment seem personal is by complimenting the color of his eyes. This works on dual levels because it allows you an excuse to gaze into his eyes for a long time.

Profession or Hobby

Compliment him about his work or hobby. For instance, if he paints, compliment his paintings. Make the compliments genuine by studying art.

Voice

When you compliment him, lower your voice slightly and lean into him. If possible, compliment him in a whispered or husky tone. Your compliment should seem like a secret or something intimate.

Eye Contact

It is recommended to make eye contact while paying him a compliment. You can also add a tiny smile with this. This will prove that you are genuinely impressed and that you are paying him a sincere compliment.

Do not go overboard with compliments. If you compliment him a lot, it will seem fake. It will reduce the impact of your compliments. He may even think that you are pranking him. A few sincere compliments are far better than dozens of fake ones.

Playfully Tease Him

Playful teasing and humor are two great flirting techniques. You just need to be careful while using them, though. Teasing is great because it creates a feeling of intimacy. It also proves to the man that you have a sense of humor. But remember, if you deal it out, you should be able to accept teasing from him as well.

Tease your man about trivial things. For instance, if you are in school, tease him, saying that he has a crush on a teacher. If he is a dog person, tell him that he loves his dog more than any other human being.

If he is good looking, jest around and ask him how his Abercrombie job is going. If he just came back from a gym, make a hyperbolic statement about his muscles. Remember not to be offensive. Never get too personal while teasing your guy. You do not want to create any misunderstandings. Never insult his appearance, his family, his friends, or his career. You do not want to alienate him.

Leave Him Wanting More

If you ever feel the conversation has started to drag on for too long, or that he appears to be distracted or bored, then walk away as soon as you can. Your conversation should never seem boring. It is better to leave while he is still interested. This will leave him wanting more.

Create an opening for the next time. Instead of dragging up an old topic, just move away quickly. Promise him that you will continue with the topic the next day.

Another trick to drive men crazy is by leaning in for a kiss and then at the last moment turning your head just to whisper a compliment in his ear.

Flirting Over Text

Text Him "Accidentally"

If you aren't sure how to initiate a conversation, you can do it by texting him by accident. To do this, you need to pretend that you were trying to text someone else but accidentally texted him instead. You can send a text like, "Oh, you are so right, but whatever, come on! Let us meet!" After a couple of minutes, message him saying, "Oh, I am sorry, the wrong person!" He will surely text you next and will start a conversation with you.

Don't Be Boring

Text messages can get boring quickly, especially if you send pointless things such as "What's up?" etc. Texts like these are highly uninteresting and boring. They will not take you far with your crush. It is recommended to be as unique as possible. Send a message only if you think that he will find it interesting. For instance, let him know about things that remind you of him, as this is a great way to initiate a conversation.

Leave Some Questions Hanging

Don't be too eager while texting. You do not need to respond to every message. You do not want to seem too eager, or he will think that you are under his control. It is recommended to respond to only a couple of things and leave some questions hanging. This will allow you to have a sense of mystery. Similarly, it will help you create a sense of passion around you, as well. It is also recommended to give him some breathing space. Do not ask him a lot of questions all at once. He should not feel hassled or bombarded with questions. It is recommended to keep the messages as short as possible. The messages should be sweet, simple, and quick.

Be Suggestive

Once both of you get comfortable with texting, it is now time to make things more interesting. A lot of simple texting will make things bland and clichéd. You need to add some passion to the texts. Things should start to heat up. You need to drop some hints to say that you are interested in becoming more than friends.

It is recommended to play safely in the beginning. Do not send messages that are too racy or sexy messages in the beginning. He will think that you are too sleazy. You can keep things sexy and cute simultaneously. For instance, send him a sultry flirting text. If he responds in the same tone, it is time to pull out the big guns. Pay him a flirty comment or compliment him. You can compliment him about his body etc.

You can be even racier by suggesting some suggestive things. For instance, you can send him a text saying that you are in the shower. Don't say anything after that, and let him imagine things on his own.

Don't Send Too Many Texts

While texting is a great way to flirt, you should never overdo it. According to the rules of texting, you are supposed to send only the number of texts that you receive. If you send a few more, then it will come off as desperation. For instance, if you send your crush 20-30 texts a day and he only responds to 3-5 of them, then you are certainly overdoing it.

You need to practice self-control, or you will come off as creepy. Do not text all the time; instead, wait for him to reply. Do not text until you have something interesting to say. If you do not have anything important to say, do not say anything. If you have sent more than two texts and have not received a reply, then it is time to stop and wait.

Similarly, it is always better to wait for a guy to send you a text. Be mysterious and bold. Act kind of aloof for a while. If he texts you, he is surely interested in you. Never send messages such as "lol" and "k" etc. These texts are atrocious because they disallow any chance to continue the conversation. They are also a pet peeve of many people. Many people find them extremely obnoxious.

Picture Text

Texting images is a great option for communication. This way, your crush will always have your picture on his phone.

You can send him a group picture with your friends and ask him to join you. Or you can send a random selfie and ask him to entertain you. You can even send him a movie poster and ask him whether he would like to go out to a movie.

Make a Date

Texting can be used to make plans, as well. For instance, if you want to ask the guy for a date but are too nervous about doing so face-to-face, you can do it in the text as well. Just send him the movie poster as mentioned above and ask him whether he would like to join you.

If he says yes- congratulations, you have a date on your hands. Now go and plan it!

If he says no, that's fine; just say, "Cool! Some other time then." It is quite easy to play cool over text. It is not as nerve-wracking as in real life.

Therefore, these are some of the main techniques and methods of flirting with the man of your dreams, as these steps are easy and quick. You just need to be cautious of one thing, though. Never overdo these things, or else your beau will think that you are desperate and are being creepy.

Chapter Nine: Seductive Body Language Techniques

In the last chapter, we saw a lot of flirting techniques that can be used to attract a man. We also covered flirting with the help of body language. But there is much more to body language than what meets the eye. In this chapter, let us have a look at some of the most common techniques that can help you to flirt with your beau.

Before moving onto the intricacies of body language and how to use it to attract and flirt with your guy, it is necessary to understand what body language is.

What is Body Language?

As the name suggests, body language means the various movements, gestures, and expressions that your body does. It is literally talking through your body. Every person uses their body to send signals to other people. These signals are varied and convey a lot of different emotions. For instance, these signals can convey messages and feelings such as repulsion, attraction, insecurity, security, annoyance, and happiness as well. It depends on the position and movement of your body parts what message you want to convey. Many times, it is simple to convey your message through your body or body language more than your words. For instance, when you are annoyed at a person or do not like whatever he is saying, you automatically cross your arms in front of you. Some people also tap their feet when they are impatient. Therefore, even though you are not aware of it, you are communicating your feelings effectively.

Along with the above feelings, body language can also convey other feelings, including love and affection. For instance, if you are interested in a man, you automatically lean towards him while talking. You may even start to mirror his actions. Your mind may not accept that you like him, but your body certainly knows that you are totally into him. You can use body language for your own benefit. Your body is a great tool to seduce men. You just need to know how to do it and what to do it.

Tips on How to Seduce Men with Body Language

In this section, let us have a look at some of the easiest and common body language tips that you can use to flirt with a guy. These are great for general seduction as well. How you use these tips depends on you.

Use Your Smile

Everyone is born with a great smile. And everyone likes to see a smiling person as well. A smile is a potent asset to attract people. How you smile and use it matters a lot. There are two kinds of smiles, the "Pan Am Smile," and the "Duchenne smile." You are supposed to use the Duchenne smile and not the Pan Am smile. Pan Am smile, as the name suggests, is the smile that air hostesses use. It is a fake smile that has no emotions behind it. The Duchenne smile is a genuine smile. You are supposed to smile with your eyes while smiling the Duchenne smile. When you smile genuinely, your partner will think that you are really into him.

Another form of the smile is the sexy smile. A sexy smile can be used to let your partner know that you are available and that you would like to do some naughty things with him.

Use Your Belly Button

This might seem strange, but it is true. You can use your belly button to communicate with the guy you like.

According to researchers, pointing your belly button toward the person you love shows that you are interested in him. It also shows that you trust this person. Therefore, even if your head is turned away, it is recommended to keep your belly button toward him.

Touch Him...But Not Too Much

Some slight touching is appropriate and needs to be done to show that you are genuinely interested in the guy. But if you keep on touching the guy all the time, he will find it inappropriate. He may even get creeped out. Keep things as "accidental" as possible. Never forget that you are supposed to be tasteful. Always do things in a subtle way.

Avoid Crossing Your Arms

Crossing your arms is a negative signal that you send toward people you dislike. If you cross your arms while talking to the guy you like, he will subconsciously think that you don't like him. Crossing your arms shows that you are not interested in the person. It also shows that you are disconnected from the present and are not interested in anything that is going on around you. Crossing your arms frequently can also show that you are insecure about something.

Strike a Power Pose

Power poses are not limited only to businessmen and women. Power poses allow you to bring your best side forward. The people who use high power poses such as hands-on-hips etc. feel more confident than people who use low power poses. People who use high-power poses tend to perform better in their day-to-day lives. This strategy can also be used while flirting. Spread your legs, keep your shoulder back, and put your hands on your hips while talking to a man. This will make you seem strong and bold.

Lock Eyes with Him and Then Look Away

It has already been mentioned that eyes are quite important if you want to learn how to flirt properly. Batting of eyes, coy eyes, eye contact, etc. are all flirting techniques that are heavily dependent on eyes. When talking to regular people such as your parents, or your neighbors, or your friend, you tend to make eye contact for a minute and then look away. This is normal. But when you want to convey your emotions and feelings of attraction, the eye contact needs to be more intense. It needs to be deeper. Don't be shy about making eye contact with the person you are interested in.

Only eye contact is not important. You also need to learn how and when to lower your eyes. Once you maintain significantly long eye contact, look down gently and part your lips slightly. This is a highly erotic move that will heat up the room. It mimics the expressions that women tend to have while having an orgasm.

Make the Most of Your Lips

After your eyes, your lips are the most important organ for flirting and seducing a man. There are many things that you can do with your lips to seduce a man. The first thing that you need to do is to wear bold colors - the bolder the color, the better the attraction. Red is the color of passion and love. But if you feel uncomfortable using a stark red lipstick, you can use a slightly subtle shade. Biting, opening them slightly, parting, batting them, are some of the many things that you can do with your lips to attract the attention of the guy you like.

Play with Your Hair to Attract Him

While hair is dead, it can surely help passion for coming alive. There are many ways to use hair to attract the attention of a man. You can:

- Toss your hair back.
- Pull it over one should while exposing your neck.
- Putting it up when he is around
- Twirling a section around your finger.
- Pick a couple of tactics and do them, but don't go overboard. It will look strange.

Show Him Your Interest Using Facial Expressions

You will be shocked to know that a person makes about 25,000 expressions throughout the day on an average. Faces are extremely expressive, and you can use them to communicate a lot of things. Sometimes your face can communicate a lot better than your voice can. You need to learn how to use your face to tell him what is on your mind.

Lean in Toward Him

Leaning towards a person shows that you are interested in him or her. When you lean towards a guy, he will think that you are interested in him and that you want to talk to him. Leaning away from someone shows that you are not interested in them at all.

Therefore, whenever he is talking, lean in slightly. His subconscious will pick the signal, and he will realize that you are interested in him.

Wear Clothes That Make You Feel Your Best

One of the best things that you can do to make your body language attractive is by being as comfortable as possible. If you are comfortable with yourself, others will feel comfortable about you as well. Therefore, if you do not normally flip your hair and feel uncomfortable about doing it, it is recommended to avoid it altogether. Instead, do something else that you are comfortable with. The same is the case with your clothes. Many times, people think that looking sexy on the first date is essential. But if you feel uncomfortable in your clothes, it will backfire hilariously.

Instead of wearing excessively skimpy and tight clothes, it is recommended to wear clothes that are clean, fit you well, and have no wrinkles. A tiny bit of cleavage is fine, but do not overdo it. Remember, you are supposed to be attractive and not sleazy.

Your clothes can make you look sexy, but nothing is sexier than a lot of self-confidence. So instead of focusing a lot on your clothes, focus on cultivating self-confidence instead.

Live In the Moment

While it is true that these tips can help you immensely while flirting and seducing people, you should not limit yourself to them. Flirting and seduction are not mechanical, they are organic, and they need to be changed according to the place and time. These tips should be used as a script for your date. Treat these tips as suggestions. You can change and adapt them according to your discretion. Honestly, if you are confident and bold enough, you can change these tips and make them suitable for you.

You cannot prepare a blueprint for a date. It will always be unpredictable. Therefore, change your strategy accordingly.

Ultimately, every woman has a different method and approach towards seduction and flirting. Every woman uses her body differently, making body language a highly individualistic subject. For instance, some women use dance to seduce men, while others use their voices. If you cannot use any of these two, then you can surely use yours. Whatever technique you use, remember to personalize it according to your needs. It is necessary to be as authentic as possible. Only authenticity will produce good results, so be authentic.

It is also recommended to think of the things that you want from the man you are trying to seduce. Do not use these steps if you are in a new relationship and are still treading the waters. If you use these tips in the initial stages of a new relationship, the guy will think that you are interested in casual hookups only.

Chapter Ten: The Official First Date - The Major Dos and Don'ts

The modern world is incredibly rapid and is like a whirlwind. Everything is fast-paced, and every new day brings in a new challenge. It has become quite difficult to find the right person. But this does not mean that the modern world has not come up with modern solutions to solve these problems.

For instance, nowadays, there are many events such as singles nights, speed-dating events, etc. that can help you find the one. The time at such events is limited. This limited time, combined with the hardships of the world, can make it quite difficult to find the right one. It is therefore recommended to be your best self all the time. You need to put your best foot forward all the time. You need to be in your top form.

First dates can be quite difficult. There are many things that you should avoid while going on a first date. Similarly, there are many things that you must follow while going on a first date. In this chapter, let us have a look at some of the most common factors that you need to consider for making your first date a successful one. If you follow these tips carefully, you will surely be able to make your first date count.

Do's

Turn Up On Time

It pays to be on time, especially on first dates. Being late is a sign of tardiness. It also shows that you do not care about the date. Every minute of delay will make your date think that you have stood them up. Sitting alone and waiting in a restaurant or a café is a traumatic experience. No one likes to go through this experience. Therefore, it is recommended to be on time. If you cannot be on time, inform your date of the potential delay.

Display Interest

First dates are difficult because you are bombarded with a lot of information. Do not expect to remember all this information. Some of the information may be relevant to you, but most of it won't be relevant or important. But this does not mean that you should not act like you are interested in the information. Feigning interest is a characteristic that everyone needs to learn. If a man puts in an effort to show that he is interested in you and talks to you about his life, then it is recommended to show at least some amount of interest in what he is saying. Even if the topic bores you to death, pay attention to him. Don't yawn!

Listen More

Everyone loves to talk about themselves. People can spend hours on end talking about themselves. People tend to do this a lot on the first date because they want to prove that they are indeed a catch. But this constant verbal diarrhea will bore anyone. Similarly, it won't help you in the long-term. A first date is an opportunity to find out things about your date. So instead of talking a lot, try to listen a lot as well. Speak less, listen more to show that you are genuinely interested in the person.

Ask Questions

If you ever feel that the conversation is entering the "silent" territory, ask him questions. The questions should be lighthearted and interesting. The questions should be asked in a way to ensure descriptive answers. Remember, asking questions does not mean interrogation. Do not ask any personal questions about your date. Similarly, avoid topics that can lead to controversies. If your date refuses to answer a question, do not force him to answer it.

Make Eye Contact

Eye contact is quite sexy if you know how to do it. Eyes are windows to a person's soul. They show your real selves. You can convey a lot of feelings such as love, honesty, and attraction through eyes. Dishonest people tend to avoid looking at people in their eyes. If you do not look into the eyes of your date, he will think that you are lying or are being dishonest. Maintaining eye contact is essential if you want to create a spark of chemistry between you. But making eye contact does not mean that you need to stare at your date all the time. Maintaining good eye contact means looking away from time to time. If you keep on staring at your date, he will find it creepy.

Be Honest

Relationships are built on trust and honesty. You cannot expect a relationship to work if you are not honest. It is recommended to be as honest as possible. Random fakery and falsifications will not work, and your lies will be exposed eventually. You should always be proud of who you are and what you are. If your date does not like something about you or vice versa, it is better to be honest on the first date itself instead of lamenting later.

Make an Offer to Pay the Bill

According to the unwritten rules of chivalry (which some men and women still follow), it is the duty of a man to pay the bill. But this is a dated and sexist concept. Instead of forcing your date to pay for you, it is recommended to offer to pay. Show your intent to pay the bill. Many men find this sexy because it shows that you can care for yourself and that you are confident and bold. If he insists on paying the bill, accept it graciously.

Compliments

There is no one in this world who does not like a compliment. While men often pay compliments to women, it is recommended to throw in a couple of compliments towards men as well. Compliments can change the tone of the conversation. They can make the conversation highly positive. It is recommended to keep compliments simple and clean. Say things like you mean them. Fake compliments will not be appreciated. Do not compliment your date just because he complimented you.

Don'ts

Let us now have a look at some of the don'ts of first dates.

Don't Talk About How Great You Are

Talking about yourself and how great you are is off-putting. No one wants to hear you talk about yourself all the time. It is true that the first date is an opportunity to talk about yourself, but it is also an opportunity to get to know your date. If you keep on talking, without giving your date any chance to speak, he will feel disinterested and frustrated. If you want the conversation to be successful, both the partners should be involved equally. Whenever you feel that you are talking a lot, take a step back and let your date speak. Remember, speak less and listen more.

Don't Keep Checking Your Phone

One of the rudest things that you can do while talking to someone is checking your phone all the time. Being on the phone all the time while someone else is talking to you is rude. It will make the person feel that you are not interested in them or are being disrespectful towards them. If you keep on checking your phone all the time, your date will think that your phone is more important than them. If you are indeed expecting an urgent call, it is recommended to let your date know about this. He will surely understand.

Don't Be Under-Dressed

It is far better to be slightly overdressed than to be underdressed. Showing up to the date, looking like a hobo, will kill all your chances of a second date. Look fresh and active. Your date will surely appreciate your looks. Showing up for the date in sweats shows that you do not care for the date and therefore did not put in any effort.

The Myth of Perfection

One of the biggest myths in the world is "perfection." No one is perfect, and you should not try to be perfect, either. It is recommended to focus on the relationship instead of focusing on how to appear perfect. Your date will surely accept you with your quirks. Truly, imperfection makes a person perfect.

Past Relationships

Many people tend to spend a lot of time talking about their past relationships on their first date. While you should never hide your past, you should dwell on it either. No one wants to hear how much you loved your ex or how much he cheated on you. If you ever find yourself in such a situation, it is recommended to change the subject as soon as possible.

Don't Think Too Far Ahead

We get it, you are looking for commitment, but this does not mean that you start planning your whole life with your date just after the first meeting. Instead of focusing on what can happen, try to focus on the current moment itself. Focus on the present and try to focus on connecting with him. Live in the moment and be happy in it.

Don't Use Cheesy Lines

Cheesy lines never work. Only horny teenagers use them, and the only place where they seem to work is shown and in the movies. They are crass, stupid, and immature. Instead of throwing cheesy lines at your date, try to develop a personality. Read more, watch more movies, and indulge yourself in various activities. These things are far better than cheesy pickup lines.

Therefore, as first dates can be a piece of cake, if you know what to do and what to avoid, this list will surely help you crack the code of perfect first dates.

Chapter Eleven: Kissing - Are You Doing It Right?

One of the most intimate, erotic, and passionate things that you can do with your partner is kissing. Kissing displays your passion, your love, and your affection. Kissing can also be quite sensual and erotic. There are many different types of kisses and kisses. The basic difference between kisses is a simple kiss and a passionate kiss. You can take your making out experience to the next level by making your regular kisses passionate. In this section, let us have a look at some interesting tips that will your kissing experience more passionate and bolder.

Stay in the Moment

A kiss does not work just on the physical level. A kiss can only become passionate when both the partners are fully present in the moment. The intentions, ideas, and thoughts of both the partners are crucial to making a kiss successful. A kiss is complete on its own, and it should be treated like this. It is recommended to be fully present in the moment. You should not use kissing as a jumping platform for other activities. Never rush into or rush out of kissing. Your kissing should open your heart to your partner. He should feel the love and emotions seeping through the kiss. A passionate kiss should be able to display how much you love him and how attracted you are to him.

Do not be overwrapped with the notion of kissing. Be mindful of whatever you are doing, but don't let kissing become too mechanical. Kissing is an activity of passion; it does not have to be a calculated activity. If you are thinking about anything else, stop it. Just focus on your object of attraction and dive deep into the kiss.

It's More than the Lips

Many people think that lips and tongue are the two organs that are involved in kissing. While this is technically true, kissing that involves only these two organs is often bland and lacks passion and intensity. To make kisses more intense and passionate, you need to involve a lot of things in the process of kissing. It is true that your lips do most of the work while kissing, but to make the process more passionate, you can mix in some sensual touches. This will heat up the room. You can also touch your partner's chin or play with his earlobes. Make them kiss as "full-bodied" as possible. You can also moan while kissing to make things more intense.

Keep Things Loose

As said above, kissing should not become a task or a mechanical process. You need to let loose and enjoy it as much as you can. Kissing should involve a lot of tongue. The tongue is highly flexible and strong. You can make it move around and tighten it at the correct places to make the feelings intense. Your passion should flow like an uninhibited stream and should drench each other. Enjoy the unending river of pleasure and ride its waves with full force.

Eye Contact is Your Friend

Eye contact can be incredibly sexy if you know how to do it. Look into your partner's eyes while approaching the kiss. This will help you convey your passion to him. Once the kissing starts, shut your eyes and enjoy the waves of pleasure.

Test the Waters with the Tongue

Sometimes, some people like the use of tongues while kissing. If your partner is one of these guys, then ask him whether he would like to use his tongue while kissing. If he agrees, use it gradually. It needs to be slow. Do not force him. Ask him from time to time whether he likes it, whether he enjoys it, and whether he finds it pleasurable. Kissing should feel natural. Pay close attention to the body language of your partner and check whether he is comfortable or not. Try to match the pace of your partner. If he is moaning with pleasure, pull him in, and do not stop. If you feel him pulling back, then slow down slightly.

Build Energy Slowly

Keep things slow! Pausing from time to time between kissing can really make things more intense. These pauses can help you convey your passion. It also provides your lips and tongue a moment of respite. Look into his eyes deeply and build up the passion for your next kiss. The slow nature of kisses will only heat things up. Gently grazing his thighs while kissing can help you make things move in the right direction.

Study Up

While it may seem hilarious, studying before kissing can really help you make your kisses passionate. There are many online tutorials, books, TV shows, movies, etc. available that can help you learn how to kiss. Pay close attention to the details and list down what you find attractive. It can be the movements, gestures, eye contact, etc. Use these details when you kiss your partner the next time.

Practice as Much as Possible

The best way to become a passionate and sensual kisser is by experimenting and practicing a lot. You can do solo practice, or you can find a partner to practice as well. For solo practice, just emulate your kiss on the back of your hand. This will help you to learn how to use your lips, your tongue, and your mouth. You need to be as confident as possible with your technique. But don't forget the passion. A kiss needs both passion and confidence to make it a great kiss.

Kissing is an essential aspect of any romantic relationship. While everyone knows how to kiss, not everyone knows how to do it correctly. You need to do it properly to make things passionate and intense. This chapter will surely help you become a great and passionate kisser.

Chapter Twelve: How to Lure Him into Bed (in a Non-Slutty Way)

Is there a man that you have been eyeing up for a long time? Are you attracted to him but do not know how to approach him? Do you drool at the prospect of getting him into your bed? But are you scared because you do not know how to do so? Then don't worry. This chapter will help you unlock the secrets of getting a guy into your bed without acting slutty or sleazy.

Approaching a man for sex is not difficult. You just need to understand the intricacies and nuances of the art of seduction. It is not rocket science. It is quite easy. You just need to be confident, bold, and strong; everything else will work for you just fine.

Here are some easy to follow tips that will help you learn how to pull a man into your bed. These tips will put you on the right track towards your dream guy. Remember, these tips are a form of guide for you. You need to put in the details according to your needs and requirements, as well as the circumstances.

Don't Be Too Eager

There are proper times and places for everything. Do not be too eager to lure your man into bed. If you feel that things are mellow and cold, you should refrain from approaching the dream guy. No one likes people who are too into them. If you appear too creepy, clingy, or "horny," your dream guy will think that you are a freak, and he will run away. Men love the feeling of the chase. They love the adrenaline rush. They want women to play a little hard to get. They want you to make them envious. Men dislike women who come onto them all the time. A little chase will boost their ego and will always help you to get him in your bed.

Feel Sexy

To be sexy, you need to feel sexy. Sexiness is attractive. It attracts people toward you like a magnet. Sexiness is not related to your beauty; it is much more than that. If you are confident about your sexiness, you will ooze it. Think about your best features whenever you approach someone. You need to feel sexy to act sexy and be sexy as well. Your sexiness should be so seductive that every guy you approach should want you. You should be able to feel desirable all the time.

Be Flirty

Flirting is a great way to show a guy that you are interested in him. You need to tease the guy and make him jealous. Do not be obvious about your attraction toward him. Your attraction should never be obvious. He should feel that you are interested in him, but the interest is temporary. If a guy ever thinks that you are in his control, he will stop caring about you. Your chances to get into his pants will become negligible. He will make you his plan B. You should never become someone's plan B.

Focus on Building the Tension

Sexual tension is essential if you ever want to sleep with your dream guy. This can only be achieved with the help of various gestures and body language. Stand close to him whenever you want to talk to him. While talking casually, brush your arm against his.

Expose a side of your neck by putting your hair to one side casually. Whenever he makes you laugh, touch him gently. These are some of the most potent ways to build sexual tension. What we say with our words matters, but what we say with our bodies matters more. Let your body do the talking for you.

Don't Hang Around

If you are at a bar or at a club and your dream guy approaches, then have a casual chat with him. But do not tail him throughout the night. It is true that you do not want him to go home with anyone else, but if you follow him around all the time, it will make you seem creepy. Similarly, it will prove that you have your eyes set on him. This will reduce his interest in you. To avoid this, enjoy your night. Dance with your friends. You need to show your beau that you do not need him; rather, he needs you.

Make Him Compete

This means that you need to show him that there are other men who are interested in you. Men love to chase and compete. Show him that he is not the only one who is after you. If he approaches you, greet him casually, and indulge in small talk. In this conversation, point out how other men are interested in you. This needs to be done in a diplomatic and subtle way. If you act too harshly, it will ruin your chances forever.

Create an Opportunity for Him to Approach You

Men do not like approaching women when they are surrounded by people or are in a group. It is quite an intimidating task to approach a group of women, especially if they are confident and sexy. If you are with your group all the time, your dream boy will never approach you. To prevent this, go to the bar alone and have a drink. You can also dance alone, away from your group for a while. Allow him some space to approach you on his own.

Make Eye Contact

Eye contact is incredibly sexy and bold. It is one of the best ways to flirt. Make and maintain eye contact with your dream boy from time to time. Do not overdo it; just a couple of times is fine as well.

When men look at women, the first thing they notice is their face. They do this so that they can check whether a woman is interested in them or not. Eye contact is the best way to let your man know that you are indeed interested and want him as soon as possible.

Don't Give Him Everything

So, you did manage to get him in the bed? Congratulations! But wait! Do not hurry. It is understandable that now that you finally have your dream guy in your bed, you just want to rip off his clothes and have a passionate night of lovemaking. But if you do this, he will not come back for more. If you are making out passionately, pull back from time to time. This will help you enhance the passion and the intensity of the moment. He becomes enraged with passion, and his desires will become bolder. This will surely make him come back for more all the time.

Use Texting to Your Advantage

If your dream guy asks for your number or if you have text in the past, then you are on the right track. Texting may seem to be a bland form of communication, but it can be incredibly sexy and naughty as well. If you really want to get the guy in your bed, just be naughty and a little cheeky. Tell him what you are wearing or let him know what you want him to do. Let him visualize what he would like to do with you. This method can be used when he is around you or is far away from you. It will drive him crazy with passion.

But Don't Over Text

Remember, men love the chase. If you act too sleazy and desperate by texting him all the time, his interest in you will wane quickly. Let him make the first move, even if you desperately want to get into his bed. He should feel the same desperation that you are experiencing. If you have sexted in the past, pull back and act friendly. Play it cool for some time. He will put in more effort, which will make the whole thing sexier.

The Yes Game

If he does decide to make love to you, then brilliant! But wait; don't say yes right away. Remember, men love the chase, and now that he has approached you with his intentions, he is under your power now. You need to learn how to control him now. Play hard to get to make things even tenser. Do not give him whatever he wants right away. Enhance the sexual tension to make lovemaking even more passionate.

If You Just Met Him, Don't Text Him

If you have just met your dream guy at a party and you exchanged numbers, let him make the first move. Do not call him or text him either. If he is really interested in you, he will surely text you first. Remember, men love the chase. Be nonchalant about things and let him do things at his own pace.

These tips have been tried and tested. They will surely help you get your dream man in your bed in no time. Just remember to keep things classy and not act desperate. Save the sluttiness for the bedroom, please!

Chapter Thirteen: When Flirting Goes Wrong

Flirting is a great way to attract the attention of the person you like. While flirting is generally harmless, it can lead to some problems if it is not done correctly. In this chapter, let us have a look at specific issues that are associated with dating and flirting.

Internal Dating Obstacles

Many times, singles complain a lot about a lot of external factors that they find problematic about dating. These include weird dates, weird ideas as presented by dates, the problems associated with online dating, the problems associated with meeting new people, the fear of rejection, and many more. There are also many other things that tend to block us from dating successfully. Many people ignore these things. These things are essential if you want to make your date successful. In this section, let us have a look at the pitfalls associated with dating.

Negative Self-Talk

How you feel about yourself and your self-esteem is important if you ever want to succeed in your life. How you feel about yourself directly affects how you feel about yourself. If you treat yourself properly, everyone will treat you properly as well. Similarly, if you treat yourself badly, you will be treated badly by others as well. This is a vicious circle that is difficult to escape. If you feel that you are unattractive, it will be reflected on your face, and you will genuinely start looking unattractive. Remember, confidence is all about faking until you make it. You need to become your own cheerleader. You need to focus on things that you love about yourself and ignore other things.

Taking No Action

Another problem that is often associated with dating is becoming passive or not taking any action at all. This happens when you are already in a relationship but is also seen in people who are single. These people lament about their singlehood but don't do anything about it. They don't go out to meet people; they don't join any dating sites either. They just like to wallow in their own sadness. Most of these people tend to blame the world instead of taking responsibility for their own failure. It is necessary to be accountable for your own actions.

Limiting Beliefs about Dating, Relationships & the Opposite Sex

These people tend to have negative ideas about dating. If you regularly think about how much you despise men, how awful dating is, and how each relationship is bad, then you will never find a positive relationship for yourself. Your thoughts are reflected in your life. If you want positive things to happen in your life, you need to think positively as well. Thinking positive is necessary because it makes you feel optimistic.

Excuses

We love to procrastinate. People procrastinate a lot. They tend to procrastinate in a variety of ways. You will always find a reason to avoid the task. Excuses are aplenty with people who love to procrastinate or are in general lazy.

Past Baggage

Everyone has baggage that they carry with them all the time. The only difference between happy people and sad people is that happy people keep their baggage locked and shut away while unhappy people display it all the time and lament over it. It is better to live in the present and think of the future. It is recommended to avoid thinking of the past as much as possible.

Excessive Judgments & Expectations

Many people have a lot of expectations from their dates. When their date does not meet their expectations, these people become frustrated. They stop caring about the date. It should be remembered that no one is perfect. Everyone has their pros and cons. It is necessary to concentrate on the positive aspects of your date and ignore the tiny faults. Keep your mind open and wide.

Fear of Rejection

Nobody likes rejection, but it is a very common concept in a person's life. If you care a lot about rejection, you will never succeed in your life. Some people are so afraid of the fear that they stop dating completely. They start believing that they are unattractive, and they are unappealing. Rejection is normal and to be expected. Do not take rejections personally and instead focus on how to improve yourself.

Social Anxiety

Some people are often shy and nervous around new people. This is fine, and almost everyone faces it. Unless you feel incapacitated or start getting panic attacks, it is okay to feel nervous while meeting new people. Extreme social anxiety is real, but not a lot of people face it. If you suffer from it, it is recommended to contact a therapist as soon as possible.

If you do not have any social anxiety disorder and just have a serious case of nerves, don't worry. With practice, your nerves will go away. Don't let your feelings and emotions stop you from living your life. It is impossible to control how others feel about you or how they react, but you can surely control how you feel about yourself.

Busyness

People are often busy with their day-to-day jobs. Many people also have a lot of responsibilities, as well. But this does not mean that you should stop dating at all. Singles often feel more comfortable working instead of dating. But try to go out from time to time to keep your life from getting too monotonous and dull.

Fear of Intimacy & Vulnerability

Dating means getting to know someone and finding out things about them. It also means forming a connection with a person. To form a connection with someone, you need to show them your vulnerabilities. You need to allow people in your personal space. If you do not like people breaching your circle, or if you are an excessively private person, dating may seem quite a daunting task to you. But this does not mean that you should not try it. Take things slow and work on your dating life gradually.

Seven Flirting Mistakes Women Make

One of the best ways to start a conversation with a man and to let him know that you like him and are interested in him is by flirting with him. Flirting is useful in a variety of ways. It not only conveys your interest, but it also shows that you are confident, bold, and that you know what you want and desire. It allows the guy to see your mysterious, mischievous, and feminine side. But flirting can also backfire if not done correctly. There are many things that can go wrong while flirting. Here is a small list of things that you should avoid while flirting.

Playing Games

Playing hard to get is okay if you want to increase tension, but overdoing it is never good. Playing a lot of mind games with men will make them despise you. It only works if used in limited amounts. Men have self-respect, which often borders on ego, and they will not chase you if you play mind games all the time. If you are genuinely interested in a guy, do not feign indifference or disinterest for a long time.

Being Disrespectful

Humor and sarcasm are great ways to diffuse tension. They also act as great flirting tools. Humor can keep things relaxed. Sarcasm helps you display your feisty and sparky side to your dream guy. But both these, if used improperly, can come off as mean-spirited. Your sarcasm and humor should not offend anyone, especially the guy you are interested in. Never embarrass him in front of people. It is okay to tease him from time to time, but never overdo it, or he will avoid you.

Being Whiny

Asking for help and other similar tactics are great methods of flirting for women. Men love when women ask for help, as it makes them feel like heroes. Similarly, if the help is related to something physical, the man can put his strength and physical prowess on display. Men love to show off how strong they are. But never overdo this. If you constantly ask for help and whine about your "weakness," the guy will think you are a nuisance. Asking for help is fine; *being whiny and entitled is not.* While asking for advice or help, do not complain about your friends, family, job, or other people in your life. Keep everything simple and limited.

Being Too Clingy

Guys like to have their boundaries set. They like to be "lone wolves." They do not appreciate women who act too clingy or possessive. While some amount of possessiveness is cute, too much of it can ruin a relationship. A small gesture such as a gentle brush of fingers or arms is seductive, but clinging to his arm all the time, especially when he is trying to socialize is cringy. This is especially true if you have just met him. Do not act too clingy or envious. If you start getting too jealous, he will think that you are a neurotic person and will move away from you.

Coming On Too Strong

Along with clinginess, you need to avoid coming on too strong as well. It is necessary to be mindful of the things you say, but it is also important to know how to say them. If you come onto a guy too hard, he will believe that you are interested in a hook up only and do not want anything else. Similarly, making a lot of jokes about hooking up, or sexual jokes, will make him think that you are there for sex only. If you are looking for something serious, then it is recommended to take things slowly and let them develop gradually.

Time of Flirting

Everything has a proper time and place. Similarly, there are good times to flirt, and there are bad times to flirt as well. If a guy is looking excessively sad or extremely angry, it is recommended to steer clear of him. You should avoid flirting if he looks frustrated. Anger, frustration, and similar feelings distract people. The guy will not be able to concentrate on you or your advances. He may even react negatively to your flirting. In some cases, flirting will make him smile and therefore improve his mood. So, it depends on the circumstance and time whether to flirt or not.

Flirting in a Professional Setting

You should avoid flirting in a professional setting at all costs. This includes flirting in the office, at office parties, or professional meetings as well. If you flirt on such occasions, people may think that you are a sycophant; this may affect your career negatively.

Flirting Backfire

Flirting is a great way to introduce yourself to new people, but flirting can backfire sometimes. Everyone uses flirting to get things done with ease. For instance, a simple, flirtatious smile while bargaining, or a flirtatious banter with a barista, etc. Some women also use specific, and seductive lilt of their voice to ask for help.

People who are experts in the art of flirting know how to bat the eyelashes and cast suggestive looks to get things done for them. They can use these methods to find allies, friends, and social power. It is recommended to use each tool you have in your arsenal to get ahead of everyone. It is highly efficient to use your weapons when they are needed.

Erotic capital and prowess can really change the game for you. These are two gifts that can be used to get whatever you want, whether it is physical, material, or mental. Erotic capital is a combination of social as well as physical attractiveness. Flirting is one of the many techniques that are associated with this capital. Charisma and charm are a part of flirting that is appropriate and recommended for all kinds of situations.

While it is true that flirting can help you sometimes, it won't always help you. It can even backfire if you are not careful. For instance, flirting makes you vulnerable to judgment and misunderstandings. People can form misperceptions about you. It can even lead to a social backlash, as well. Experts believe that flirting is good for business, but it involves taking a lot of risks that can lead to various problems as well.

Flirting suggests the possibility of something sexual that may happen between individuals. It expressed with words, with the pauses, tone of voice, the posture of a person, eye contact, wordplay, gestures, and body language. Harmless flirting can help you a lot, but if the context of the flirting is not understood or if it is misread, then harmless flirting may evolve into something totally different. For instance, flirting in a bar is different than flirting for getting out of a speed ticket.

Many women tend to use flirting to get out of difficulties, such as a speeding ticket. While it is a tried and tested method to get away for free, some policemen may feel insulted by the obvious flirting and manipulation. Therefore, instead of getting away for free, you may land into even more trouble. It may even get you arrested.

The workplace often sets the scene for misunderstandings, as it is often easy to misconstrue intentions and ideas in the workplace. Many employees tend to employ flirting with improving their chances of getting a promotion or getting in the good graces of their employers. Similarly, many salespeople try to use the art of flirting and cajoling to attract customers. But if this kind of flirting is misread or misunderstood, your credibility may come under fire. People may even start to question your character and your intentions, as well. It will surely break down the trust between you, your employers, and your customers. In worse case scenarios, you may get fired, or a complaint may get registered against you. Therefore, many experts do not recommend workplace flirting. It is always better to keep things simple and professional at a professional place.

Some other experts believe that workplace flirting can work wonders. If the person who plans to flirt is an expert at flirting, he or she will not get into difficult situations. These experts believe that flirting only backfires for people who cannot flirt properly. Such people lack good judgment and do not possess the skills required to flirt efficiently. To flirt successfully without creating any problems, a person needs to understand the situation, time, place, and the person he or she is trying to flirt with. Only then can he or she flirt properly without any problem.

But then other professionals believe that sometimes even experts fail. While an expert flirter is well accustomed to his or her style and method of flirting, the opposite party may still feel objectified and insulted. This is a serious problem at workplaces because reputation and respect matter a lot in such big organizations.

Ultimately, flirting can make things extremely difficult for you if you do not know how and when and where to do it. Flirting blurs the line between your intentions and what you say. This may confuse a lot of people, which may lead to misunderstanding. Misunderstandings can lead to grave results in professional settings. Therefore, it is recommended to avoid flirting in the workplace and reserve it for bars and clubs only.

Chapter Fourteen: But, Is He Mr. Right?

If you have been dating a man for a long time, this question is bound to come into your mind soon. This question has plagued a lot of women since the beginning of time. It is a serious question that has only two options. This infamous question is, "Is he serious about me?"

Women are constantly plagued by this question due to the lack of connection between men and women. Men do not understand the feelings of women, while women don't understand what men want. Women get confused about what men want because often men do not know what they want for themselves, and this confusion is reflected onto women. Due to this confusion, women tend to overthink and scrutinize even the smallest details. This hair-splitting activity leads to a lot of stress and undue pressure. When this happens, women tend to lose all their hope about a new, budding relationship. They start thinking that they will never get a man to stay. They also become suspicious of men's intentions and judge them all the time. This is why it is better to form a connection with your boyfriend as soon as possible.

Many times, it so happens that when you start relaxing and enjoying the bliss of a long-term relationship, the guy you are in love with starts to become distant. He starts to move away gradually from you. When this happens, women start to relive every living moment of their existence just to check what they did wrong. They tend to recheck every sentence, every word, every action, and every object that they ever said or experienced with their man. This is done to find the root cause of the problem - but usually, all this exercise is in vain.

If a man is serious about you, he will display it through his actions. But rest assured, if he does not show this, it is not because you did something wrong. If a guy does not want to commit, it is his problem. There is nothing wrong with you. Men tend to be indecisive about a lot of things. Many times, they do not know or understand what they really desire due to a multitude of options. But instead of being suspicious of them, it is recommended to give them their time and space to come up with a decision on their own. If you feel that they are taking too long, wait some more. If still, he does not want to commit, maybe it is time for you to have a serious, life-changing talk.

When men are serious about you, they will flaunt it with pride. They will let you know that they are genuinely serious about you through their actions, gestures, words, expressions, etc. You can observe whether a man is serious about you or not by observing his or her behavior. By observing these signs in his behavior, you can save yourself from unnecessary trouble, pain, and overthinking. You just need to pay attention to his behavior. Here is a small list of 20 things that men tend to do when they are serious about you. If your man displays most of these signs, then congratulations, you are in for the long game.

Priority

Men have a lot of things going on in their lives. This is especially true if the man is a career-oriented person. Still, if you are his number one priority, then rest assured, he is serious about you. What does being someone's number one priority mean? It means that the man will always have time for you, even when he is busy. He will refrain from making excuses about not talking to you or meeting you. He will tend to go out of his way just to meet you. If he is really interested in you, he will try to make things happen in such a way that he and you will be together all the time. He will not lie or use excuses while talking to you.

Deeper Level

As said above, many women are plagued with the question, "Is he serious about me?" This question has ruined a lot of lives. It is a classic problem that seemingly has no solution. But there are certain things that can help you to solve this question. Whenever you think "Is he serious about me?" start thinking instead about, "Is he *curious* about me?"

If a man is curious about you, then he is invested and interested in the things that are going on in your day-to-day life. He wants to know your likes, your dislikes, your fears, your passions, things that make you nervous, things that you prefer, your favorite food, your favorite book, your favorite TV show, etc. He does not want to know these things just for the sake of it; he wants to know them because he is genuinely interested in you and wants to get to know you better. He wants to understand you on a deeper level and is therefore serious about you.

He Listens to You and Asks for Your Opinion

Men are lone wolves; they rarely take advice and suggestions. Therefore, the classic "not asking for directions" stereotype has been perpetuated so much. Men are often bad listeners, as well. So, if you see your man listening to each word carefully and hanging onto them, then you can be sure that he likes you and is serious about you.

To make the deal sweeter, if he asks you your opinion about things, especially in his personal life, then it means that you mean something to him. He appreciates your ideas and thoughts. He wants to understand your perspective on some levels because he respects you and loves you.

Listening is one of the easiest ways to check whether a person is interested in someone or not. You can never force a person to pay attention to something, especially if they are not interested in it. This is why if a man is paying attention to you and is waiting for your advice, then he is a keeper. He is surely serious about you.

He Trusts You

Trust is a crucial aspect and the basis of relationships and dating. Without trust, no date or relationship can survive. Without trust, it is impossible to form the foundation of a healthy relationship. But testing whether a man trusts you or not can be slightly complex. If done incorrectly, for instance, pranking him with a "cheating" prank can break his trust forever. Instead, there are many simple, obvious, but often ignored ways that can be used to check whether a guy trusts you or not.

If a guy trusts you, he will be honest and open with you. He will feel comfortable talking about his fears, feelings, emotions, and similar things with you. He will be honest with you and will let you know things about his life. If he can be honest with you, then he trusts you with his soul. If you are the first person with whom he shares his life-events, then he surely loves you and is serious about you. He wants to share things first with you because he wants you to understand how special you are.

You're Spending More and More Time Together

In the initial stages of a relationship, couples tend to spend a couple of hours with each other every other day. The time you spend with your partner is based on a lot of things, but on average, in the initial stages, the number of meetings is few, and the duration of meetings is less.

In the initial stages of a relationship, couples tend to meet for just a couple of dates per week. But with time, the intensity of the relationship increases, and the couple starts to meet more and more. They start to spend more time together. This is also an indicator of the man being seriously into you. If he were not into you, he would have escaped long ago. If he initiates the dates himself, then rest assured he is crazy for you.

If the guy is not interested in you, he will make many excuses to avoid spending time with you. But if he goes out of his way and cancels stuff just because he wants to be with you, then rest assured he is really into you and would like to take things further. This man is a keeper, and you should not let him go.

He Pays Attention to Little Details

Women are extremely meticulous. We have a fine eye for detail. We pay close attention to things that often go unnoticed by men. Therefore, they cannot tell the difference between mauve and lavender. This does not mean that men are born without the ability to perceive details. They do, but it is just that they do not find them interesting enough to retain. A man's mind does not care about minutiae; he only pays attention to details when he is seriously invested in something or someone. Therefore, if your man remembers all the important dates, your favorite things, your complex coffee order, or notices things like a simple haircut, then he is serious about you. He notices these things because he is observing you. And along with the observation, he is also paying attention to minute details, the things that are happening in your life, and what is important to you.

He Keeps His Promises

Men have traditionally been associated with the role of heart breakers. These "bad boys" do not care about anything and are notorious for breaking their promises. While these are some unfortunate stereotypes, men do not consider promises to be important. Women are more likely to keep promises as compared to men. But as said above, relationships are built on trust and mutual respect. If your beau keeps his promises all the time, then he surely cares about you.

If he promised you to take you to dinner at the end of the week and follow it through, then you are in luck. Many men who are not serious tend to break their promises by making random excuses.

They try to get out of their promises. Nothing is sexier than a man who can keep his word and can stick to his promises. Such men never disappoint anyone because they know that promises have feelings and emotions as a base. Even if he screws up (after all he is a human being), he will apologize profusely and will try to make it up to you.

He Shows His Love with Actions

If a man is serious about you, he will not only say it. He will always try to prove it to you through his actions, as well as his gestures and body language. He will appreciate you and will shower his affection on you as well. He will also comfort you whenever you feel sad or depressed. He will try to surprise you and will make you coffee in the morning. He will do anything just to see you smile. He understands that his proclamations of love are useless if he cannot follow them through and act upon them. This is why he will always be ready to try and prove his love for you as well.

He's Excited About You When You Aren't Around

A guy who is serious about you tends to talk about you all the time, even in your absence. If your friends and family complain to you all the time just because your boyfriend talks about you all the time, then he is surely in love with you. A man talks about a woman all the time because he is genuinely interested in her, and she is on his mind all the time. Many times, men fall in love with a woman's absence. If he goes crazy whenever you are not with him, it means that he has fallen for you and is in love with you.

He Makes Plans with You in Advance and Sticks to Them

If a man is serious about you, he will make plans in advance and will always try to think of new ideas to have fun with you. He never worries you about things. He is never absent. He will always have something planned for your entertainment. He makes your life exciting and worth living. No matter how busy he is, he will try to find time for you. He will make plans with you and will keep the plans as well.

He Always Looks for Ways to Include You in His Interests

He shares your passion with you. He also shares your hobbies with you. He looks out for you. If both of you are interested in two distinct things, he tries to incorporate you into his activities, and he tries to participate in yours as well. He does not keep things to himself because he likes to share things with you. He wants to be an integral part of your life and vice versa as well. He tries hard to understand your passions, your interests, and your hobbies as well.

You've Met His Friends and Family

If a guy is serious about you, he will want you to meet his parents, family, and friends. In fact, if a guy wants you to meet his parents, then it is the ultimate sign that he is really interested in you and wants to take things further.

If a guy takes you for granted or tries to gaslight you, then he will never want you to meet his parents. He will refrain from meeting his family and friends as well because he has no intention of staying with you.

If he does let you meet his parents, then he is genuinely in love with you. It also means that he is proud of you and wants to share your presence with everyone. He wants people to know that he loves you and appreciates you. He wants everyone to know that you are the one who is meant for him.

He Treats You Like a Lady

A man who is genuinely in love with you will always treat you like a lady. He will not make you wait, and if he does, he will apologize profusely. He will always treat you with respect. He will always open doors for you. If he ever commits a mistake, he will ask for your forgiveness. He will never rush you into things. He will appreciate your decisions. He will never force you to do anything that you are not comfortable with. Your happiness and respect are his number one priority. He treats you like a lady because he knows that you are a lady. He wants you to feel like a lady, as well. He wants you to feel proud of him. He wants you to feel safe with him.

He is Punctual

A guy who is genuinely interested in you will try to be punctual. He will try to be on time for dates. If he ever arrives late, he will apologize. This shows his respect and cares for you. If a man does not care for you, he won't even try to be on time. He will never apologize if he ever arrives late. If a man is not serious about someone, he does not care for them. He does not feel that he should apologize to a person about whom he does not care because there is no sense of attachment present between you and him. Men possess empathy, but it is often selective.

He Regularly Initiates Contact with You

He calls you first, sends you random texts, and promises you that he will call later when he misses your call. You do not need to worry about his manipulative behavior because he never manipulates you. Similarly, he does not lie to you either. He does not make any excuses if he messes up. Rather, he apologizes in an honest manner. He initiates contact with you, and you rarely must wonder where he is. He likes to tell you about his plans for the day. He informs you well in advance if he isn't available for a long period of time.

You Have Fun Together

If his eyes lit up when you are with him, and he genuinely laughs at your jokes, then he is really interested in you. He genuinely cares about you and appreciates you a lot. He does not act reserved around you, and similarly, he does not play hard to get. You should not play hard to get, either. You feel relaxed with him, and whenever you are going to be absent from each other, he always appreciates you for spending time with you.

When a man is serious about you, he looks at things from a different point of view. He wants to enjoy the relationship and have a lot of fun with you. He wants to be your partner in crime. He enjoys things and likes spending time with you. He is not just interested in having sex with you, but he is more interested in being with you. This is the main difference between men who are genuinely in love with you and those who are faking it just to get into your pants.

He Talks About Future Plans

Everyone likes to talk about their future, but if a man talks to you about his future with you, then he is serious about you. He is genuinely interested in you and wants to spend the rest of his life with you. He does not take you for granted. Every second that he spends with you matters a lot to him. He is happy to spend time with you and envisions a future with you. He wants to go on long journeys with you. He is not just focused on the present, but he wants to spend time and discuss the future of your relationship as well.

He Shares Everything with You

A guy who is serious about you will share his dreams, his thoughts, his ideas, and his fears with you as well. If something angers him, he does not try to confront you. Instead, he thinks about the incident calmly and talks to you about it. He considers your opinion on the matter to be crucial. He encourages you to be open to him as well. This is how the relationship thrives and survives properly.

He Tries to Resolve Arguments

No relationship is perfect, and each couple goes through ups and downs all the time. In fact, many people say that if a couple does not fight with each other, they are not true love. Couples are bound to fall into arguments frequently.

Now that it is settled that every couple fight, why should you care? The main factor in this argument is not that all couples fight, but rather *in the way this fight is resolved.* All couples fight, but the difference between successful couples and regular (or failed) couples is that successful couples solve their problems properly. The guy who cares about you will deal with the arguments properly. A guy who is serious about you will try to solve the problems without letting them escalate. The guy who loves you will not make you feel bad or sad about the argument. He will not insult you just because he is mad at you.

A guy who is serious about you rarely loses his temper with you. Even if he loses his temper, he will never insult you. He will pick his words properly because he knows that he does not want to lose you ever.

He's Open about Your Relationship

Whenever you meet his friends or colleagues, he introduces you as soon as possible. He never misses any chance to introduce you to his friends or family. He is proud of you and is open about your relationship as well. He wants the whole world to know that you are dating each other. He always holds your hand when you walk together.

If other girls ever show interest in him, he declines them politely by letting them know about your existence. He tells everyone that he is taken immediately.

Therefore, if your boyfriend shows some or all the above signs, then rest assured, he is serious about you. Now you do not need to worry about whether your boyfriend loves you or not. He is a keeper and wants to be with you forever.

Chapter Fifteen: 25 Seductive Hacks to Keep Things Juicy Long Term

The media all around us always talk about how women can have better orgasms, better sex, or a better relationship. These sources also come up with various tips to do so. But these tips rarely work because they do not understand the intricate nuances of the female psyche and thinking.

Many times, we love our boyfriend or partner. But love does not equal a healthy sex life. Quite often, sex may turn into a regular ordeal if you do not know how to spice it up. There is nothing worse than sex becoming boring. Keeping your sex life active and healthy is essential for any relationship to survive. Not many people know that this is a common problem. Sex tends to become predictable and routine, often in a long-term relationship. The intensity and the chemistry that is present in the initial stages of a relationship fades away with time. While it is true that it is impossible to go back into time to relive those moments, it does not mean that you cannot bring back the passion once again. In this section, let us have a look at how you can spice up your sex life to avoid it from becoming routine and boring.

Initiation

Long-term relationships bring with them a lot of things, such as comfort, relaxation, love, and calmness. But they also make partners take each other for granted. Partners stop making any effort to feel more attractive and keep the relationship exciting because they already know that the relationship is not going anywhere. This pattern also gets repeated in your sex life.

Women are often stereotyped as coy and coquettish. They are not expected to initiate sex often. But this is an old stereotype. If you want to keep your relationship and sex life active and exciting, you need to break the boundaries and destroy the stereotypes.

Initiating sex should not seem like a task. For instance, many people initiate sex at the end of the day when both the partners are already exhausted and just want to sleep. Therefore, sex becomes a task or a "before bed" activity. To spice things up, initiate sex at random moments, especially when your partner does not expect it at all. For instance, initiate it in the morning right after he gets out of the shower or while he is tossing a salad. This will surely spice up your sex life.

Be a Tease

Being a tease and acting playful can really make your sex life pop. Being a tease does not require a lot of time or preparation. Simple dirty talking is one of the best ways to be a tease. Men love dirty talk. Try dirty talking at inappropriate places where sex is impossible, for instance, while dining out or while in a theatre. This will keep things exciting and will drive him crazy.

You can also do this during sex itself. Quite often, sex becomes a routine task for long-term partners, which is why they end up hurrying. They just want to get it over with. Instead of doing this, you can prolong the sexual activity by teasing him as long as he can stand it. Get him on the brink of orgasm and then hold back. Wait, and continue. This will drive him crazy and will make things absolutely sexy for both of you.

Surprises

One of the best things to keep a relationship exciting and fun is the element of surprise. To keep the fire burning, try to surprise your partner from time to time. Get back home before your boyfriend sometimes, and as soon as he comes back, take him straight to the bedroom. You can also welcome him wearing nothing but your birthday suit. Beware and ensure that he is alone before you do this.

Plan a Romantic Weekend Getaway

Surprise your boyfriend with an impromptu trip just for the two of you. Vacations are expensive, and often time-consuming, but it is not difficult to do one on a limited budget. It is fine if you can afford just a night away. Even a single night vacation can work wonders for your relationship. Your partner will surely appreciate the effort and thought that you put into the trip. He will also enjoy the change of scenery. And there is surely nothing better than spending some quality time with your loved one.

Wear Lingerie

Lingerie can really spice up things for you, especially in a long-term relationship. When we are in a long-term relationship, we tend to let go of ourselves. Both the partners start wearing random clothes, sweatshirts, ratty tees, etc. While this is a great thing as it allows you to be cozy and comfortable with each other, it kills the sexual intensity and attraction. Lingerie can help you light the fire once again. You can surprise your partner with a new set of lingerie or ask him for help while buying one. Enter the bed while wearing a sexy, hot negligee and invite him to your bed. Or, slip into something seductive while he is watching TV and crawl into his arms. Lingerie can make things spicy for both partners.

Pretend to be Strangers

This is another way to spice up things. It has been shown in many popular shows as well. If you have a good sense of humor and both of you can act (no need to follow Stanislavski), you can act like strangers meeting for the first time. Meet at random places or meet where you had your first date. In this method, you need to pretend that you have just met for the very first time. Seduce each other and hit on each other.

Take Charge for the Night

Another thing to make things sexy is by taking charge of the night. By taking charge of things, this means taking control of everything. Make all the decisions and lead him into them. If your boyfriend does not like being passive in general, he will surely enjoy this change. It will allow him to relax and take things slowly. Have your way with him and take your sex and relationship to the next level.

Let Him Be in Charge

You can make things spicy by doing the exact opposite of the last tip. Let your boyfriend take charge of the night. To make things kinkier, tell him that you will be his servant tonight and will allow him to do whatever he wants (do keep in mind that both of you still need to respect each other's boundaries."

Props

You can use many kinds of props to spice up your seduction game. For instance, wearing lacy lingerie and teasing him using the laces can bring on the game. Similarly, you can use melted chocolates, strawberries, etc. to heat things up. Eating strawberries slowly and seductively while holding eye contact is incredibly sexy and erotic. You can also eat melted chocolates. Don't be scared to get dirty.

No Hands Rule

You can make the foreplay interesting by bringing in the no-hands rule. For this rule, the man can do things, but he cannot use his hands. Tease him throughout this game and watch him moan with pleasure. Your man will come up with many different creative ways to follow this rule.

Text Dirty

Texting is a great way to seduce your man, especially at inappropriate times. For instance, if he is at work, send him a sexy text and tell him what you plan to do with him that night. This will keep him on his toes throughout the day, and the anticipation will make things spicy at night.

Send Pictures

Nudes can be classy too! Instead of sending him random pictures of your genitals or breasts, make them erotic and seductive. For instance, a transparent top or a short skirt that barely covers your buttocks will make you look sexier than being in your birthday suit. Click some pictures wearing these clothes, in suggestive posts and forward them to him. He will be flabbergasted and will rush home soon. Beware of sending these photos to casual lovers because you never know when they may just turn up on the Internet to haunt you.

Take Him Shopping

Shopping can be quite a boring task for many men, but this does not mean that you cannot use it for the purpose of seduction. Ask him to accompany you shopping. He will act grumpy and mean, but gradually take him into a lingerie shop. You will see his frown changed into a large smile, and his eyes light up. Offer him some sneak peeks from the trial room. Whisper in his ears about the lingerie.

Seductive Looks

In a long-term relationship, sex often gets boring. Partners stop caring how they look. Quite often, people wear pajamas, buns, and sweatshirts. But breaking the monotony can help you spice things up. For instance, occasionally, dress up for him in your best clothes. Look sexy with slight makeup, sexy hair, and clothes that leave nothing to the imagination.

Undress

Once you show him your clothes, now it is time to show him what is underneath. Clothes are like wrapping paper, while your body is his gift. Act clueless and seductively while slowly removing your clothes. Stripping casually but seductively is one of the best ways to seduce a man.

Foreplay and Tease

Intense foreplay can help you keep things heated. Give him everything and lead him on, only to break the play before the final act. Tell him that you are going for a shower, or just excuse yourself by saying that you have work. This will enhance his cravings for you. He will feel frustrated and will moan with passion.

Shower Together

Sneak casually into the bathroom when he is showering. Do this when he expects it the least. Showering together is incredibly sexy. A sexy shower will make your mornings brighter and bolder.

Leave your Fragrance

If you have a favorite fragrance, use it as an asset. Spray it around in certain places that will remind him of you. Your aroma will surely tantalize him. Don't overdo this, though, as some people may find it irritating.

Create the Mood

Creating the mood for sex is not difficult. Playing seductive and romantic music, lighting scented candles, wearing a negligee, decorating your room with flowers such as red roses, etc. are easy ways to set the mood of the room. You can also personalize the room by adding things that are special to you. For instance, certain items may trigger memories of good and sexy times.

Be His Masseuse

Massages are incredibly relaxing, but they are also incredibly sexy. Give him massages frequently and touch his erogenous zones. For instance, bite his earlobes, kiss his throat, touch his navel, etc. Touching erogenous zones can make a man go mad with pleasure.

Plan a Romantic Weekend

This is another extension of the vacation plan. If you cannot plan a vacation, plan a romantic getaway. Surprise him with a simple stay at a luxurious hotel. This will not only enhance your sexual relationship, but it will also make your emotional bond stronger. Making emotional bonds strong is as necessary as a strong sexual relationship.

Play Strip Poker

Another thing that can make your sex life more interesting is by playing strip poker. There are various versions of strip poker available online. You can also personalize strip poker according to your needs. Let your creative juices flow.

Roleplay

Roleplay is a great way to heat things up in the bedroom. Share your fantasies with him and ask him to share his with you. Also, ask him which characters he loves, and which stars he finds the hottest. Then, one day, surprise him by roleplaying his dream character. Use your acting and makeup skills to attract him and make the illusion stronger.

Touch Him in Public

Touching in public is a great way to make him go crazy with passion. For instance, when you are eating out, move your naked feet over so they touch his leg. Or gently touch him under the table and then touch yourself. Winking, raw kisses, etc., will drive him crazy as well. Don't go overboard and keep things under the PG level while in public.

Try a New Position in Bed

Try out some new positions in bed. You do not need to choose the difficult ones that require the precision and flexibility of a yogi or a contortion artist. Just be yourself and guide him through this new experience. There are many easy positions available online, so check them out.

Learn a Few Erotic Moves

Dancing is incredibly sexy unless you are born with two left feet. Making the right dance moves will make him go crazy. To make things sexier, wear sexy attire, and learn some seductive moves online. You can also add some stripping to make things sexier. Remember, seduction is about hiding things and revealing them one by one.

Therefore, these are 25 tried and tested ways that can help you charm and seduce your man. The art of seduction is not complicated, but it requires some practice. You need to be charming and playful. A lot of charm and a lot of eroticisms will make your man go crazy with pleasure. Remember, it is more about hiding and not about revealing. You should always leave him wanting more.

Plan your game properly and follow it carefully, but don't be afraid of changing things or breaking the rules if it means infinite pleasure. A little creativity and a little boldness will make your bedroom a room of pleasure.

Conclusion

Flirting is a bold and huge topic. It entails a lot of things that cannot be covered in such a small book. There are many different facets associated with flirting that makes flirting so complex. Flirting is a highly cultural thing. It changes from culture to culture. In fact, it can change according to the region as well.

This book can really work wonders in the lives of single women. If you do not feel confident about flirting with a man, the methods and techniques mentioned in the book will help you to attract your crush.

The chapters given in this book have been tried and tested. They are bound to work. The instructions given in this book are easy to follow. Anyone can follow them.

Confidence is essential for any job. If you are not confident, you won't be able to flirt with the man of your dreams successfully. Therefore, a detailed chapter on confidence-building has been covered in this book.

Flirting works on multiple levels, out of which physical and verbal are the two most important levels. Both levels have been covered extensively in this book. A detailed chapter on body language will help you achieve your goals with ease.

Remember that flirting is supposed to be an organic thing. There is no blueprint for successful flirting; still, the tips provided in this book should be used as stepping-stones.

Due to these and many other qualities, this book is surely one of the best books about flirting available on the market. Women who use the methods given in this book are sure to find a high-value man and will spend the rest of their life with him knowing *how to keep him interested.*

Reference

https://www.mookychick.co.uk/how-to/how-to-guides/how-to-seduce-like-cleopatra.php
https://www.cosmopolitan.com/sex-love/a23583489/passionate-kisses/

Part 2: Get Your Ex Back for Women

The Ultimate Guide on How to Start Dating Your Ex-Boyfriend Again and Get Him Back, Including Relationship Advice to Keep the Love Alive

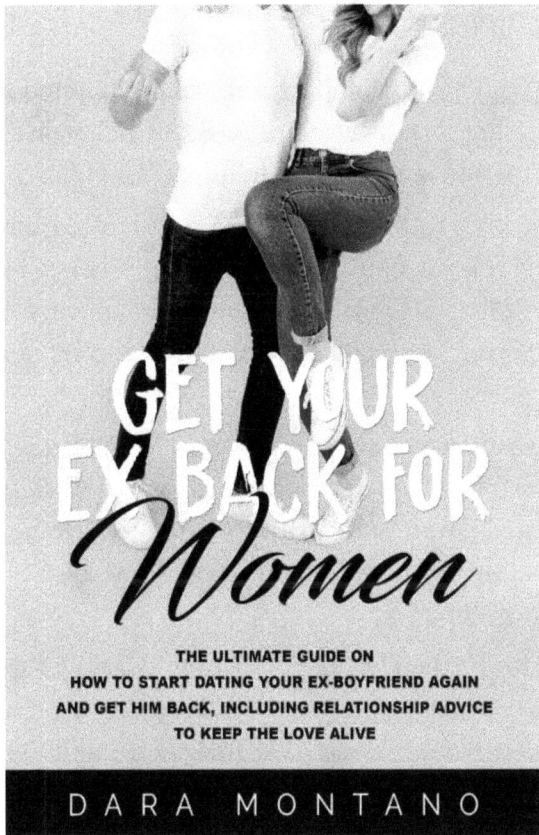

Introduction

Love is one of the most significant and profound emotions of human beings. Feeling loved and having a sense of belonging are essential requirements for a meaningful and fulfilling life.

While there are various kinds of love, most of us eagerly seek love in a romantic relationship more than the others. The need for emotional and physical connection with a romantic partner could be inherent. However, the ability to form a strong and sustained relationship is learned.

Scientific evidence suggests that our ability to form stable relationships starts in our infancy, which is the first and foremost bond that we make with our caregivers who feed, clothe, and protect us. So, we all work hard to create and establish long-standing romantic relationships.

Yet, breakups happen frequently as well. Breakups are *never, ever fun*. Breakup periods are marked by anger, tears, messy night outs with people you would never have imagined going out before the breakup, emotional eating, and everything else horrible and agonizing that fit between the listed items.

If you are reading this, then it means you seek help, and seeking help is the most effective way of solving problems. This book contains a 5-step formula that has worked wonders for many women who have successfully gotten their exes back, including me. Yes, the ideas and suggestions given here are based on personal experiences.

When my boyfriend broke up with me, I thought my life was over. My initial reaction was that of absolute shock, and I lived like a zombie and automaton for a week, not even believing that my relationship is broken - lying to myself that he would be back home soon.

But, even after a couple of weeks when my boyfriend did not return, I realized it's really happening. Then, I started the second phase of my breakup session. I stopped going out, preferring to spend time alone and "mourning" over my breakup in different ways, especially binge-eating and binge-watching romantic TV shows.

Suddenly, I decided I needed to do something about it. But, instead of taking things slowly and calmly, I started sending him highly emotional texts; first, "begging" him to return, then "threatening" him, and then groveling so much that I felt disgusted with myself. Nothing happened, except the pain of the breakup got excruciatingly agonizing, and I was sinking into despair.

It was during such a low period in my life that my best friend came to my help. She first brought me back to reality and showed me the way to stabilize my life, after which both of us started looking out for relationship experts who can help me get my ex back. I tried many of the tricks and tips that were shared by numerous experts. Some seemed to work well for a while before turning sour, some others did not even take off, and some others had a reverse effect and drove my ex further away from me.

Confused and bewildered by the multitude of tips, options, and suggestions from various sources, I decided to take a step back and study each of these methods in detail. I made copious notes of my journey, writing down my experiences, thoughts, and emotions as I tried as many ideas as possible, eliminating those that did not work, fine-tuning those that worked, and more. I filled many books with the outcomes of my direct experiences and the learning I had from them.

After I got my ex back, I had forgotten about these notes. I was reminded of them when another friend approached me for help with a nasty breakup she was going through. As I delved into my notes and tried to steer my friend's get-back-my-ex journey, I realized I have a treasure house of experience-based knowledge that can help many others out there.

It is easy to understand and relate to people who share my philosophy of life and help them get back on their feet during tumultuous times, just like how others helped me get back on my feet. This book is a rich resource of lessons learned from my direct personal experiences as well as those whom I have tried to help.

It is easy to connect with your sense of helplessness, desperation, and rage; when you feel powerless to do anything about a breakup, you know deep in your heart is not right. This comprehensive roadmap will guide you through your difficult but possible journey of getting your ex back not because you "need" him, but because you deserve each other, thanks to the limitless love, affection, and concern you have for each other.

As you read, you will find helpful and resourceful answers to the following mind-numbing questions:

• How is it possible to get your ex back when you don't even know where to begin?

• Why is a courageous, objective, and creative outlook critical to get your ex back?

• How to handle the stubborn attitude of "I need my ex back, and I will do anything to get him back."

• How to win (or balance) the power struggle in any romantic relationship, broken or otherwise?

• How to make your relationship happy and meaningful after you get your ex back?

The most important thing for you to remember as you start on your challenging journey is to know that you are not alone. This book will be your guide as I share my experience of starting out as doubtfully as you are doing right now and finishing off with a great flourish. My ex is now my husband, and both of us feel happy in a relationship that is far more enlightened and meaningful than it was before the breakup.

So, go on and start your journey as you equip yourself with relationship techniques and skills that will not only help you get your ex back but also aid in enhancing the strength of your relationship.

SECTION 1: Breakup Psychology and Survival

Understanding and clarity of thought is the trigger to finding solutions to any problem in the world. The same holds good for breakups too. If you don't know what went wrong, how can you ever begin to set things right? Therefore, taking a step back ward is essential to moving forward.

If you want to fight the battle to get your ex back, the starting line is understanding the breakup psychology followed by surviving the initial few days, which can really be a struggle. There is no doubt that the first few days will be a struggle. However, with some help, especially from your own grit and determination, it is possible to overcome these challenging days and come through not unscathed but stronger than before.

Let us start with why relationships end.

Why It Ended

Reasons for breakups are not only numerous, but each type of breakup can have layers of differences depending on the existing psychology of the relationship, as well as the mindset of each of the individuals, not to mention a multitude of external factors that you may never be able to control.

Interestingly, some relationship breakups can happen for very frivolous reasons. For example, neither of the partners can't pinpoint what went wrong. One of the partners decided to break up for no apparent reason. The lack of self-awareness could be an underlying reason in such cases.

For example, counselors are known to come across couples who break up because the man in the relationship said, "I broke up with my girlfriend because I believed I didn't like her anymore."

Before we go into the various reasons why breakups can occur, one critical point to remember is emotional reactions (sometimes, even seemingly unreasonable to you) are normal. After all, emotions are an integral part of human relationships. While all of us usually welcome "happy and positive" emotions, we like to avoid negative ones. However negative emotions are as normal and typical of human beings as positive emotions.

Therefore, instead of avoiding negative emotions and finding fault yourself or your partner when these apparently unpleasant situations driven by negativity arise, it is better to accept them as a normal and healthy aspect of any relationship, including yours. Following are some common reasons for relationships to break.

Individual differences - In the honeymoon period of any relationship, only similarities between the partners get all the attention. All kinds of differences are not just tolerated or relegated, they are sometimes even encouraged, either in the hope of taking the relationship to the next level, or out of fear of losing the relationship. Healthy understanding and handling of differences are not part of the honeymoon period.

Yet, like all things, the honeymoon period ends, and the "real relationship period" kicks in, and that is when disagreements and differences begin to show their "real" faces, leaving both partners unprepared to handle them well. Most couples experiencing a "real relationship" tend to:

• Think that they have made a mistake while choosing their partner.

• Have an increased number of conflicts.

• Blame each other for each of their own problems.

• Think of "breaking up."

A situation like the above usually means that neither of the partners has learned to treat differences with respect, find ways to defuse or manage conflicts, accept each other's differences, and solve problems. In such situations, the partners have not yet taught themselves to be generous and kind despite all the apparent differences.

Lack of focus in the relationship - While it is true that relationships need to be worked on, in the initial stages, it is more important to focus on the relationship and pay attention to each other and their needs. Frequently, couples start relationships with a sense of satisfaction. However, soon both end up taking each other for granted and stop focusing on the other person's needs and requirements. When partners stop paying attention to each other, then:

• They feel disconnected from each other.

• They don't indulge in physical touches and embraces anymore, excluding indulging in the sexual act.

• They don't do things together anymore.

Additionally, the pile-up of normal stresses of living a life together has little time and energy for intimacy and romance. Consequently, partners increasingly spend less effort on the relationship. Worse still, they hold grievances against each other until there's nothing left to do but break up.

Interestingly, most counselors agree that when couples seek professional advice in one of the above two cases, the chances of working out differences are very, very high.

Difficulty in influencing each other - Another common reason for breakups is when there is a perceived lack of balance in the relationship. When either partner feels he or she is giving more than the other to the relationship, it may be that neither can influence the other.

In any relationship, both partners must change dynamically to fit and accommodate each other's needs. A healthy relationship involves the continuous changing of partner roles and life experiences. If one of the partners ends up changing almost all the time, then resentment and anger are likely to creep into the relationship.

Other miscellaneous reasons - The above three reasons are the most common ones that end up breaking a relationship. There could be other miscellaneous reasons as well, such as alcohol or substance abuse, unresolved childhood trauma, and physical or mental health problems.

These reasons are far more complex than the three common ones, and it becomes exceedingly important for the "healthier" partner to tread carefully in the relationship. The miscellaneous reasons listed enhance the risk factor of a breakup.

One of the most common ways that men handle their breakups is to maintain a physical and emotional distance, and one of the most typical methods of breakup handling of women is to remain friends. The following two reasons primarily cause the reason for this huge behavioral difference between the two sexes:

• The basic nature of handling emotions in men and women is different.

• The role of relationships in a society and how they feed our individual sense of self-worth.

As a parting thought on this section, it is important to know and remember that men and women deal with breakups very differently. You already know that men and women feel pain and agony during breakups. However, men handle their pain very differently from women.

Interestingly, multiple surveys have revealed that the self-esteem of both men and women increases when they are in a happy, stable relationship. Therefore, both sexes lose out during a breakup and undergo identity conflict and a sense of loss. However, the type of loss that men and women experience is different.

Typically, in a relationship, the sense of being paired up with a woman boosts a man's self-esteem. A woman feels connected in a relationship from which she derives her self-esteem. It is, therefore, natural for men and women to handle breakups differently, considering that the basic needs of every relationship vary considerably.

Men, traditionally speaking, handle the pain of a breakup by being socially active and by avoiding being alone. Women are more likely to depend on close family and friends to cope with their pain. Research again shows that men need to "do" something to numb pain, whereas women need to "connect" with people to get the same numbness.

For example, you are likely to find women who have just had a breakup sharing a cocktail in a huddle made up of close friends and family in which the most intimate details of the breakup are shared. Men, on the other hand, are likely to go on an adventure holiday with friends, bury their heads in work, or get online in search of a new relationship.

Typically, most men deal with breakups through one or more of the following ways:

• He ignores his ex-girlfriend completely, cutting off all contact with her.

- He jumps headlong into a new relationship.

- He always chooses to behave badly with his ex-girlfriend.

- He has numerous one-night stands with different women.

All these behaviors can confuse and confound any woman who is trying to get her ex back. It is easy to think that he did not care about her at all during the relationship and has absolutely no regard for her after the breakup. A woman is likely to wonder whether a man who is behaving so erratically is worth having back at all.

If you doubt his actions, you must remind yourself that all his reactions have nothing to do with you. They reflect his own pain of the breakup and how he is feeling inside. The realization of this truth will prevent confusion in your head and help you focus on staying strong and find and follow your path to recovery. Let us discuss some of the common reactions of men who are writhing in breakup agony and don't know to keep the pain from driving them crazy.

He cuts off all contact with you - Cutting off contact is a way of brushing the negative emotions under the carpet so that he doesn't have to deal with them. He is not avoiding you, merely trying to preserve his mental wellbeing and sanity.

He is behaving like a jerk - If it looks like he is behaving like a huge jerk, then it is quite likely that the breakup is having a huge toll on his emotions. The bigger the jerk he becomes, the worse he is feeling about the breakup. Being a jerk is one of the most common ways men use to deal with negative emotions.

He has numerous one-night stands - This attitude of his might seem like he is getting over you quickly and effectively. However, he is desperately searching for something that will help him recover his sense of self-worth and self-esteem that he has lost with the breakup.

He jumped into a new relationship almost immediately after the breakup - Let us look at two scenarios in this case. Either he dumped you for a new relationship, or you dumped him immediately after which he found a new girlfriend. The latter case is like the one-night stand; your ex is trying to find something desperately to recover his lost self-esteem.

In the former, perhaps, you should acknowledge that he found someone while he was with you and quickly got into the new relationship after breaking up with you. Again, the important thing for you to remember that all these reactions are about him and not about you.

As a woman, you probably feel vulnerable and open to a lot more emotional angst than a man. Yet, your ability to face the harsh truth empowers you with the strength to handle a breakup better. So, what if you got a little over-emotional and raved and ranted more than he did. It is still a better way to release pent-up emotions instead of ignoring them or pretending they don't exist.

Regardless of his reaction, you must stand your ground, face the reality of the day, and identify ways to stay strong and come through the difficult phase unscathed. The first and the only person who you should focus on after a breakup is YOU. There is little doubt that women are better equipped to handle pain than men. So, let's use this advantage and get our lives back in order instead of moping around.

Should You Want Him Back?

When you are hurting deeply because of a breakup (regardless of who made the first decision to break the relationship), you are thrown into an area of discomfort, not to mention the pain associated with a breakup. When confronted by discomfort, the natural human tendency is to get back to the earlier comfort zone, and that means getting your ex back.

You feel that the pain and discomfort you are currently experiencing will go away if you can manage to get your ex back into your life because then, your life will be back to "normal." Even though these thoughts exactly what you are thinking while undergoing the hardship of a breakup, it is the gist of your core thoughts.

Therefore, a brutally honest question to ask yourself is this, "Should you want your ex back in your life at all?" This question is valid for both scenarios, namely:

• If your partner broke up with you and is now pursuing you to reinstate the relationship

• If you broke up with your partner and now want to get back with him

In both cases, you must have rational answers to the question, "Should you want your ex back?" The answer to this question could be simple and straightforward.

Your relationship could have been a beautiful one that had abundant love, affection, and unconditional support for each other. Regardless of who initiated the breakup, it is likely that you admire, trust, and miss your ex. The reason for the breakup could have been a temporary lack of focus and attention to the relationship.

The breakup could have acted as a wake-up call for both partners, and they would have realized that being back in the relationship is the best thing for both partners. It is natural for people to get confused and be uncertain about things for a short period, and then the realization of the value of the relationship might hit them like a bolt from the blue. And then, the person who initiated the breakup realizes how he or she was insensitive enough not to anticipate the pain caused to the other partner.

Moreover, frequently, breakups happen when there is a sudden drop in emotional attraction, which might have returned to its original state during the breakup period. There could be a multitude of reasons for a breakup to have legitimate and meaningful reasons. In such cases, wanting your ex back is not a question of "if" but "how and when."

So, if you felt loved, wanted, enjoyed the company of your ex, shared future goals together, and had a powerful sense of belonging with each other, and finally, if the breakup was just a one-off in the relationship, then it is important not to waste time on this section of the book. You are sure you want your ex back, then go ahead and work on how you plan to get him back using the tips and ideas given in the later chapters of this book.

Marriage is another strong reason for couples to get back together because it strengthens committed bonds through children, shared finances and property, religious restrictions, fear of social stigma, and sometimes, even difficulty in getting divorced. In such cases, the benefits of being together are likely to outweigh the benefits of breaking up, and couples do end up making accommodations for each other to get back together.

When your partner wants you back? - An important question at this juncture would be, "Why should I want to get back my ex, especially if he has dumped me?" Well, the answer to this question is best explored and decided by yourself and no one else. Yet, here are some pointers to help you understand your conflicting feelings:

• It takes courage for someone who has dumped you to return, apologize, and ask for another chance.

• This prodigal has probably learned a valuable lesson and does not want to repeat the mistake.

• At the time of breaking up with you, likely, this person never meant to hurt you. It was only about themselves. Consequently, you can safely assume that this person who has come back to you did not "plot deliberately" to injure you in any way.

• The reason for the breakup was to do with your boyfriend's confused state of mind.

Finally, it makes sense to reiterate that there is no "perfect" person waiting out there for you. So, if someone who has dared to own up his love for you comes to you a second chance, then maybe it is right to give it to him.

An important point to consider is whether you feel a sense of danger around the man or if you are not attracted to him. In either of these two cases, it is better not to want your ex back. Otherwise, it might be a prudent idea to take one thing at a time and give your ex a chance (slowly, of course) to prove himself before you make your decision.

When you want your ex back - Let us look at a situation where you want your ex back (with the feeling not yet reciprocated by your partner). For this situation, let us assume you are in the "no contact" stage (which will be discussed a little later in the book. At this stage, ask yourself the question of should you want your ex back and delve into your heart and mind to identify honest answers.

Remember that your partner might not want you back now. However, it is in your interest that you consider the pros and cons of having him back in your life before you plunge into the effort of getting him back. If you give in to the idea that you don't want him, then you are closing a door without checking out the opportunities that lie on the other side.

Also, it is common for friends and family to advise you not to try and get back your ex. Things like "he is your ex for a reason" will be a common challenge thrown at you. However, the fact that the honeymoon period existed in the relationship means the relationship was right, and he was compatible with you. Moreover, falling in love with somebody (unlike the short-term dates that end up in complete disaster) also indicates that the relationship is worth fighting for. Things might have taken on a downslide for various other reasons, as discussed in the previous section.

Therefore, instead of hurting and feeling desolate and depressed and wishing for things that don't have a chance of happening, treat this question as allowing you to take control of your own decisions. You are the best judge of what you want and deliberately and objectively thinking about whether you want your ex back or not is being in a position of power.

While the suggestion appears simplistic, just give it a try, and you will find yourself feeling better because of this purposeful choice. Taking a stand of decision-making instead of simply begging for and hoping for mercy will boost your confidence no end.

First, you are bound to indulge in self-talk, which goes something like, "I didn't want the breakup. My boyfriend wanted it." Allow these thoughts to run their course, after which you will see yourself looking at the relationship objectively and from all sides. Consequently, you are likely to view the breakup from all angles as well, which can be an eye-opening experience for you personally.

Some of the reasons your heart and mind will try and give you are (remember these reasons are not great ones to get your ex back):

- I love him.
- I can't imagine a life without him.
- How can I find another like him?
- He is my soulmate.
- He is the reason for my happiness.

There could be variations of the above thoughts that are playing in your mind. None of them are objective reasons. Yet, many reasons are compellingly sensible enough for you to work hard and get your ex back. Here are some of them:

The decision to break up was a rash one - Often, breakups happen because the parties tend to give up on a great relationship instead of working on them. These kinds of breakups are generally rash and not well thought through. You or your boyfriend could have said something nasty, and the emotional reaction would have been equally nasty, and he chose to walk out on you.

It was a great relationship - Your relationship was great even past the honeymoon stage. There was a time when fights did not exist, your boyfriend seemed perfect for you, and you could not stop being happy. So, if you thought this makes up for a great relationship, then you are mistaken because all average relationships have the same quality. Elements like trust, communication, respect, and honesty are what make a relationship great. So, were these elements part of your relationship? If yes, then it deserves a second chance. If no, then, too, it deserves a second chance so that you get an opportunity to include these elements into a relationship and see progress.

You have a child together - There is an anonymous saying that goes something like this, "Spouses can divorce each other without much thought. However, parents require to put in a lot more effort before giving up." A divorce or a breakup can be very hard on the child, and if there is even an iota of a chance to get back together, as a parent, you most likely have a responsibility to make that effort.

Your close family and friends believe in your relationship - Most of the time, close family and friends would tell you to forget the pain of a breakup and quickly move on even if they may not always be right. However, if this same group of people thinks that you should try and get your ex back, then it means your relationship was worth something.

You see potential in your relationship - This last one is a bit tricky. After all, "being in love" makes you believe that the relationship is worth a thousand chances, let alone a second chance. Yet, your belief in the relationship is worth giving a thought. See if you can identify potential things in your relationship that counts for a great future together. If there are even two elements that you identified other than "being in love" or anything else with the potential to change without warning, then it makes sense to try and get your ex back.

The trick in getting a meaningful answer to this all-important question is to remember not to put your ex before your own happiness. Primarily, the most compelling reason to want your ex back in your life should be because you deeply believe in giving your relationship another chance and not because you "need" him.

Also, it is important not to be obsessed about getting your ex back. Spending your entire life in pursuing a man who has not even acknowledged your efforts is an idea that should be trashed. Try getting back with gusto just once. If it does not work despite all your efforts, then you must move on. You mustn't waste away your life on some false hope or a lost cause.

Understanding Men: Their Wants, Whys and Trust Issues

Have you ever wondered if your boyfriend thinks of you as much as you think of him? Well, if you did, then remember that you are just like most other women who also have similar thoughts. Men and women think quite differently, and even though there is no right or wrong of thinking, women are generally frustrated when they don't understand the thought process of their boyfriend. Alison Armstrong, a celebrated author and life coach, says that understanding the way men think is critical to keeping a relationship strong and sustained.

Differences between men and women - So, what are the differences between the way men and women think? Alison Armstrong opines that when a woman is happy, then there is a kind of vibration in the middle of her chest. When a man is happy, his neck, shoulders, and chest areas are filled with energy. He can literally puff up and look bigger when he is happy. The energy of happiness flows through his arms and result in common gestures like a high-five or jumping up to hit a crossbeam.

Another important difference is in the perception of love. Women base their decisions on love. For example, if two people love each other, then getting married is the next logical step for a woman. On the other hand, for a man, love is just one of the many factors that he considers while deciding. His goals and his vision for his future life play a big role in his decision-making.

Considering that a man does not typically expect a woman to change or give up something in her life when she is in a relationship with him, this idea of wanting to get his priorities right can be very important for a man. A man will listen to a woman's dreams and hopes and then ask himself if he can help her realize those dreams. In the same way, a man wants his woman to envision his future and help him achieve his dreams. For a man, it is not only love but also the understanding and support of his woman that rules a great relationship.

A third difference lies in multi-tasking skills of a woman. Women find it exceedingly difficult to focus on one thing and give it their undivided attention. Therefore, it is natural for women to multitask. Men, on the other hand, are not great at multitasking. They can pay attention to only one thing at a time.

For example, if a man is washing his car, and you are talking about going to a party that night, then he is not going to remember your words. It would be futile to fight with him later about his forgetful attitude. He simply was not paying attention (because he does not have the skill) to you when he was busy washing his car.

Interestingly, the desire to be loved, to belong, to have self-esteem - all of which are part of the core desires of any human being - connects men and women. You must remember that your boyfriend is not cut off from his feelings. It is just that they respond to feelings differently. Here are some more things that will help you deal with men and their thoughts:

Men accept all compliments as being true. Women, on the other hand, will think twice about a compliment they have received. Men will never think of it as a lie. Each time you compliment him, he will appreciate you for it. Therefore, praising men when they do a great job is one of the best ways to keep them happy.

Men are easier to impress than women. Ridiculous as it may seem to you, it is quite true that men are easily impressed with women who don't hesitate to flirt back with them. The thing is that they know and sometimes even try to be wary of it. But, frequently, they can't help themselves. Therefore, when you see your boyfriend flirting with someone, before getting jumpy and hyper about it, think calmly and tell yourself that he is behaving just like a man!

Men are brought up to believe they are protectors. They simply have not been able to let go of their attitude of the hunter-gatherer days. This attitude does not die even after being married for several years, and he knows that you are perfectly capable of looking after yourself.

What do Men Want? - So, men clam up, give monosyllables for answers, try and solve problems when all you want is for them to listen to you, and do a myriad of annoying things. What is it that men really want? Here are some more things that men look for in a romantic relationship:

They want loyalty. Men want women who are loyal and who will stick with them during good and bad times. They want women who will have their backs. Interestingly, it's the same kind of expectation that men have from friendship.

They want women to have faith and confidence in them. Men find a lot of comfort from their partner's belief in their capabilities. It makes men braver and stronger than before and drives them to give their best.

They don't want women who try to change them. Men are happy with whatever is available and are also willing to accept other people, including their girlfriends, the way they are. In the same way, they want women who will accept them as they are without trying to change them.

This can be a big challenge for most women because they tend to take time to commit themselves to people who are wired differently from them. So, they tend to divide men into two sections; things they like and things they don't like. The latter section is invariably subject to change - which men detest.

And the biggest put-off for men is when women use criticism to try and change them. Criticism makes men feel they are not wanted and drives them away from the relationship. The man who gets criticized chooses to give and involve less.

Roland Warren, an inspirational and revered commentator on fatherhood, says the difference between men and men is more about style than substance. He says that people are made of three layers of existence, including physical, emotional, and spiritual. Men typically engage with the topmost layer, which is the physical layer, and don't live life deeply.

Women, on the other hand, tend to quickly get connected to the lower emotional and spiritual layers where real intimacy takes place. It is not that men don't want to dip into the lower layers. It is just that they are more focused on ensuring they don't appear weak or competent, and consequently, avoid dealing with worries and emotions.

For example, suppose you say, "Honey, we need to have a talk," which is a benign statement, right? However, your boyfriend is likely to open out his shields and take cover in silence or even escaping from the situation using lame excuses. Also, the topic you discuss should be aligned with the surrounding environment.

For instance, taking up the issue of his alleged affair ideally should not happen when both of you are making dinner. Tax issues or other financial matters can take place here because they are no emotions involved, and he will willingly discuss the matter. The thing to remember is to include important issues or problems as part of a natural conversation with your man. Treating discussions of issues as an "event" is a strict no-no for men because they are simply not skilled enough to handle it.

Also, it would be good for you if you can be sensitive to the kind of questions you ask your boyfriend. Questions that can easily be answered with a "yes" or "no" should ideally be avoided. Instead, ask open-ended questions like, "What are your worries in life?" or "When do you feel happiest?" These kinds of questions tend to drive men into their emotional and spiritual layers and find answers.

Another mistaken idea about men is that they find successful women intimidating and unattractive. It is not the success of the woman that puts off the man in the relationship. It is what value he is adding to the relationship that matters to him. When his lady appreciates him and praises him for the work he does, the man has no problem being with a successful woman, even one who makes far more money than he does.

And finally, these differences are taken in general terms. Everyone is different, and your man needs not fit the bill that is described above. It is up to you to try and find out what your man wants and work at giving it to him so that you can get him back without losing out on your self-respect and dignity.

Men and Trust - Trust is a very important element in the mind of men. While you attempt to show your unconditional love towards him and demonstrate your inability to live without him in your efforts to get your ex back, remember that he is not interested in seeing your love and neediness. Or rather, he is not going to be impressed with the ideas.

In fact, men tend to feel overwhelmed when women use emotions excessively. Experts suggest that women could start journaling, which is an excellent way of releasing pent-up emotions. When they are free from emotions, then they can focus on how to regain their ex's trust through credible actions and behavioral changes.

Men are keen on seeing if they can trust you to be able to stand by them in good times and bad. Without trust, men find it difficult to commit themselves to anything or anyone, including romantic partners. Men need to see that you are ready to make changes to work at the relationship again before they decide on coming back to you.

For men, trust is based on *action*. So, he must be able to see you act out your behavioral changes in terms of physical looks, accepting and correcting past mistakes, etc. Your actions and the tangible outcomes of these actions that your ex can see are what will help you regain his trust.

Gaining your ex's trust through actions is a time-consuming process. Therefore, it is important that:

• You reflect on yourself and your earlier behavior

• You become mindful of your emotions and how you react to them

• Make detailed journaling notes

• Arrive at a sensible way of trying and getting back your ex by building trust

Take your time. In fact, you mustn't rush through the exercise of trying to get back your ex. This process involves not just getting your ex back but also enhances your self-awareness, which, in turn, builds self-confidence. You make positive changes in your life that promises not only to make your relationship stronger than before but also enhances your personal mental and emotional strength.

Is Cheating Forgivable?

We have spoken of the importance of trust in any relationship and how if you want your ex, then you need to behave and act in a way that regains lost trust. So, it goes to say that violation of trust is a primary cause of breakups. Infidelity, cheating, and unfaithfulness can wreak havoc on a relationship. In fact, multiple surveys and reviews show that cheating is the primary cause of divorce cases and pre-marital breakups.

Also, infidelity results in multiple other problems, including domestic violence, depression, suicidal tendencies, and more. You would think that these adverse consequences - especially the potential breakup of a beautiful romantic relationship - should deter people from cheating on their partners, right? However, the reality is quite contrary. According to some surveys, infidelity is prevalent in about 20-25% of marriages.

Despite knowing the adverse consequences of cheating, why do people cheat? Why risk the most important aspects of their life? What are the motivations for people to cheat? Recent surveys have come up with eight primary reasons as to why people cheat.

Falling out of love - When there is a deficit of love in any relationship, then there is bound to be infidelity. The imbalance happens when one partner is happy with the amount of love in the relationship, whereas the other partner needs more of "love" or at least demonstrations of it. The latter partner invariably goes in search of "deficit love" outside of the relationship, and the former feels cheated when he or she finds out.

Moreover, the exhilarating feeling of love that happens in the initial days of "falling in love" is naturally going to wane. The first levels of excitement, passion, and adrenaline rush that you get even when you get a simple message on the phone will wane. The intensity of the feeling called love also fades over time.

Some people tend to mistake this reduction of excitement and passion as "falling out of love." It takes some time to realize that the relationship goes deeper than this phase. During the intermittent period, cheating becomes easy and attractive to some people.

Feeling anger - Many people use cheating as a way of punishing their partners or exacting revenge driven by some feeling of hurt or pain.

For example, you might have just found out that your boyfriend cheated on you by sleeping with someone else. You are angry, hurt, and bitterly pained. It is natural for you to think that your boyfriend must go through the same pain that you experienced. This retaliatory attitude is also a big reason for people to indulge in infidelity.

Sometimes, infidelity driven by anger can happen for other reasons, including:

• Anger because of the frustrating behavior of either partner when he or she refuses to or does not appear to understand the needs and desires of the other partner.

• Anger because of a continuously absent partner, perhaps because of work-related travel or other family issues.

• Anger after a heated argument.

Irrespective of the cause of it, anger is a hugely powerful motivator for partners to cheat each other.

Situational forces - Every act of infidelity need not be premeditated or driven by dissatisfaction or unhappiness in the existing relationship. External factors like social situations wherein people just ended up drinking more than their capacity and then being thrown into a situation that they found difficult to control played a role in infidelity.

Therefore, a simple and easy opportunity to cheat enhances the chances of cheating. Of course, this does not mean that everyone who gets an easy chance will cheat. This factor only increases the motivation to cheat. Suppose you are dissatisfied in your current relationship, or perhaps, just had a serious argument with your boyfriend in which he has insulted you quite badly. You are already in the throes of humiliation and the lack of self-esteem. Now, suppose good-looking colleague comes and says to you, "I feel attracted to you because I think you are beautiful and are a great professional. Let's get a drink tonight."

Now, the chances of something happening after the drink are very high, right? This is a classic illustration of situational factors.

Lack of commitment - For some people, the lack of commitment they feel in their primary relationship becomes a reason for cheating. People with commitment issues generally tend to cheat their partners. Also, each of the partners can have different ideas about the status of their relationship. One might feel that it is serious, casual, or exclusive, while the other might feel the complete opposite.

Moreover, it is also possible one partner truly likes being in the relationship but has a problem getting into a serious commitment. Frequently, such people deliberately cheat so that they can use it as a reason to get out of the relationship, which, by the way, they might want to stay in. Other commitment issues can be in the form:

• Not wanting to commit to long-term relationships.

• Desiring only a casual relationship.

• Not wanting to be in the relationship anymore.

Unbalanced sexual desire - Frequently sexual desires of both partners are not at the same level. One might want something more than what is happening in the current sexual scene of the relationship, which is seen as reason enough to cheat. Unmet sexual needs are commonly cited as reasons for people to go in search of the shortfall elsewhere.

Feeling of neglect - When one partner feels a sense of neglect (which is like the lack of love), then this person goes out in search of attention through infidelity.

Feeling of boredom - Frequently, infidelity happens simply because there is boredom in the relationship. There are no other issues or problems except that one partner is thoroughly bored.

Boosting self-esteem - Having an affair seems to help boost self-esteem for many people. It seems like a counterintuitive thing. However, many people believe having extramarital affairs boosts their ego.

So, now the question is, "should cheating be forgiven?" There are no easy answers for this, and it is entirely yours and your partner's prerogative on whether you choose to forgive or not. However, one thing is certain that without forgiven, getting together can't happen.

Again, it might make sense to revisit your reasons to want your ex back in your life. Are those reasons good enough to cover forgiveness too? Typically, if you are looking at wanting your ex back or your ex wants you back, then somewhere deep within the partners, there is scope for forgiveness. Each of you simply need to delve deep and harness the power and courage to let go and find great reasons to get back together rather than cry over spilled milk.

Yes, it takes an immense amount of courage and willpower to forgive. But once you've done it, you are bound to be released from the relentless burden of carrying regret and resentment that is part and parcel of not forgiving. So, forgiving is good for you as well. However, it is time to reiterate that the call is entirely yours and your partner's, and both of you know what is best for you.

Regardless of whether cheating is forgiven or not, what you must not forget to do is be accountable for what happened (even if you were not the one to cheat) and analyze as to why either of you resorted to cheating. You should use this knowledge to plug gaps in your relationship and ensure these unpleasant situations do not recur. And lastly, remember that forgiving your cheating partner does not mean you are condoning it. It only tells your partner that you value the relationship more than anything else, and he *better prove his worth* when you choose to give him a second chance!

Breakup Recovery Essentials

Now that you have an idea as to why and how your relationship broke up, you should focus on self-care, taking back your physical, mental, and emotional strength. After this, it is time to set goals and work out strategies needed to get your ex back into your life.

If you are not careful at this stage, then the unresolved detrimental effects of a breakup can negatively impact your physical, mental, and emotional wellbeing and health in the long run.

Accept the reality - There is no doubt that breakups are horrible, and surviving it is extremely agonizing and painful. The worst part of a breakup is that your boyfriend has left you, but your memories about him would remain etched in your heart and mind. So, while the pain might seem to ebb a bit, whenever you see an object or person that reminds you of your ex, the flood of pain returns with a vengeance.

While there is nothing you can do about the pain, you can accept it as reality. Remember that this emotional upheaval is a process that must be experienced. Don't beat yourself up needlessly, thinking that you are taking longer than necessary to get over the struggle. Accept that it is going to take time to regain your emotional and mental stability. Remember to go easy on yourself.

Avoid bottling up your emotions and pain - It is common for people experiencing breakups to bottle up their emotions because they think the feelings will go away if ignored or suppressed. They avoid talking about it and use multiple ruses to appear normal and fine. They will keep themselves busy even while all the negative energy is piling up in their minds.

It is important for you not to fall into this trap. Unacknowledged and unresolved emotional pain will not go away; they are likely to remain buried and explode at the least unexpected time. If these negative emotions are not handled right now, you are likely to carry their effects into other aspects of your life, including the next relationship.

Therefore, you must talk about your feelings with people you trust. You can choose your best friend, a trusted family member, or even a professional therapist. If you don't want to talk to others, then you could think of journaling your thoughts. Write down everything about your relationship, along with the details of the breakup and associated emotions as well. Transferring your thoughts onto paper will not only reduce stress but also help in making your plans to get back your ex.

Cut ties temporarily from your ex - It is important to cut ties from your ex through all modes of social media. Don't try to check-in to see how your ex is doing, what he is posting, etc. These pictures and posts will not only remind you of him needlessly but also could unleash a new set of emotions, especially pictures that show him as being happy without you.

Also, put away all those objects in and around you that remind you of your ex: his clothes, gifts he gave you, or anything else. Put them away where you can't see them so that you can avoid unnecessary pain. Consequently, you will find the time and energy to focus on yourself and rebuild your life without your ex.

Avoid dating other men - Some girls try to use this ruse to get over the pain of a breakup. They believe that if they date other men, not only will the memories of their ex fade, but they will also take a boost of confidence. Dating other men immediately after a breakup is like trying to fill up that hole in your heart.

What happens is you are cultivating a habit of seeking validation for yourself and your behavior. Therefore, if you don't get this validation you are seeking, then you are going to feel even more disappointed and miserable than before.

So, instead of going after new men, it is best to give yourself and your heart and mind time to heal and recover from old wounds. It is best to try and rebuild a joyful life regardless of the presence or absence of other people. When your mental and emotional wounds are healed, then you are ready for other men, if needed. Now, dating other men will not be about "filling that hole" but about having fun and enjoying life. This joy that you have created on your own will make you highly attractive and desirable to people, including your ex, when you meet him again.

Identify and follow a hobby - A "good" outcome of a breakup is the increase is the amount of free time that you will have for yourself. Don't waste this precious commodity in moping around excessively by reminding yourself that matters are only going to get worse if you wallow in self-pity. Identify and follow a passion.

A hobby is an excellent way to refocus your resources on things that will make you happy and feel good. Dust off your old keyboard, guitar, or another musical instrument that you haven't touched for many years; sign up for a dance, yoga, or a martial arts class, which is excellent for releasing negative energy even as you use it as a fitness regimen.

Indulge in activities that give you a sense of fulfillment because it will remind you that there is a lot more to life than just your boyfriend and relationship. This is the best time to restart an old passion or start something new. Your energy levels will be spruced up, and your self-confidence will get a big, productive boost as well. Keeping your body and mind active is essential to prevent falling into the trap of depression. When you engage in activities you like and enjoy doing, not only does the level of endorphins (happiness hormones) get a boost, but also the confidence and positivity will see a big, happy spike.

Here are some more routine tips that you must follow strictly to ensure you get back on your feet sooner than later:

Eat good, clean food - One of the most common traps that we fall into when we are struggling with the pain of a breakup is to end up gorging on unhealthy and seemingly comfort foods. Therefore, you must eat healthy foods and ensure your body gets good nourishment. Be conscious of the amount of caffeine, refined foods, and alcohol you are consuming.

Don't forget your daily exercise - Keeping some time aside daily for your exercise is crucial not only for your physical health but also for your mental and emotional health. The endorphins released during the exercise period are great mood-enhancers.

Get adequate sleep - Sleep is essential for your mind to rest as well as the cells in your body to regenerate. Fatigue is one of the biggest causes of anger and all other negative emotions.

Keep the memories of your relationship as positive as possible - If you want to get your ex back, then your relationship must have had several positive and beautiful moments. Harness the positivity from such memories and try and not think excessively about the negative aspects. Even if you do, look at them from a learning perspective and how you could have handled unpleasant situations in a better way.

Find ways to calm your mind - Indulge in meditation, yoga, or anything else you like that will help in calming your mind. Anxiety and stress-driven by a breakup can cause a lot of hormonal damage, which should be countered through exercises that will grant you peace of mind.

Reach out to loved ones - Never underestimate the power of love to help soothe frayed nerves, anxieties, and fears. Lean on people whom you trust, and don't hesitate to take the help they offer you. Remember, no one can manage all problems on their own. Everyone needs help. And seeking help is a sign of courage and strength.

Don't expect everyone to understand you - Everyone has different beliefs and ideas. It is unrealistic to expect everyone around you to understand your feelings and your ideas. You are bound to have people in your life who will blame you for what is happening. That's fine but remember not to take everyone's words personally.

It is equally important to remember that you should keep an open mind and listen to ideas that you find unfavorable. You never know which idea could hold a solution for your own predicament. The trick is to be as objective as you can towards your own feelings and the expectations and expressions of others.

Focus on what you can control - The focus of this recovery period is self-care and nothing else. For this, you must focus on things you can control and leave out what you can't. For example, don't waste your limited resources of energy and time on following up on your ex, reading his social media posts, and doing things that are not going to add any value to your self-care and path to recovery.

Set goals for yourself and work on achieving them. While the focus of this book is on your love life, you must remember that you have other lives that you lead simultaneously, like your professional, social, and personal lives. They need your attention too. So, focus on those aspects of your life and make sure that your breakup is not impacting them negatively.

When you focus on what you can control, you will not only maximize your abilities and strengths, you will also realize that your life need not revolve around your ex for happiness and joy. These elements are not in others' hands. You can get joy and happiness and meaning in life when you focus and work on things you can control.

The initial breakup period is all about this. To focus on yourself, get your emotions and life back in order, understand if and how you want to get your ex back, and then move into the implementation phase. Journaling is one of the most effective and useful ways of focusing on what you can control.

Make journaling a daily habit. Make notes of what you did well and what you did not do so well. Identify ways to make the "not-so-good" things better tomorrow. Write answers for these three questions daily in your journal:

- What are the things that went well for you today?
- What are the things that did not go well for you today?
- What are the things you need to do to make sure that tomorrow you are a better person than what you were today?

Contemplating the answers to these three questions will not only increase your self-awareness, it will also help you with self-improvement. You will slowly and steadily reach the point when you have become the same person that your ex had initially fallen in love with.

Summarily, the start of recovery from a breakup is you and only you. Focus on what you can do to make yourself a better person. Stop working on things that you can't do anything about. For example, don't worry about what others are talking about or what your ex is doing right now.

Instead, focus on improving yourself, unlearning the mistaken lessons of the past, and doing things that will set the foundation for a bright and happy future. When this is done, you can rest assured that sooner than later, your ex will want to come back to you with little or no pressure from your end. He will see what he has lost and realize his folly and wind his way back to the beautiful relationship both of you shared.

Focus on self-care and build your life back with the help of trusted friends and family. The rest will take care of itself.

SECTION 2: The Step-by-Step Method to Getting Him Back

The primary thing you must remember about getting your ex back is to know that you will have to delve deep into your heart and mind and harness the power of courage and objectivity. Without these two elements, your chances of success are significantly low. Yes, the journey is going to be tough. If it was easy, then you would not be spending time and energy doing research and seeking professional help for this purpose.

How This Method Works (and the Results to Expect)

While the process is undoubtedly tough, there is no denying the fact that success is highly possible too. With a bit of courage, objectivity, and creativity, you can easily scale this seemingly insurmountable phase of your life and revert to your original happy relationship.

Don't hesitate to look at yourself and your behavior with the right kind of perspective. Avoid getting defensive about your previous actions and behaviors. Be prepared to accept your mistakes and find ways to correct them. It takes two to tango, and the breakup could not have happened without some contribution from you. Take accountability for your role in the breakup and find solutions to make sure you don't repeat those mistakes.

With the 5-step method prescribed in this section of the book, you can rest assured if you tried hard and are truly committed to getting your ex back, you will see success. Here is an estimated timeline for the entire 5-step process to happen. Remember the word "estimated" because there are no perfect and accurate answers for such situations. It could take longer or maybe even earlier than this for you. It all depends on your personal circumstances and the actual relationship:

- No-contact period: 3 weeks or 21 days
- Texting and phone calls: 7-10 days
- FIXIT date: 5-10 days after achieving a good relationship through texting and phone calls.

So, before we go into the details of the 5-step process, you might want this question answered: Will this process work for you? And the answer is an emphatic yes. This 5-step process will work for you because it is founded on correcting mistakes and building new-found credibility in yourself as well as approaching the problem in the right way.

To reiterate, one of the primary reasons for the breakup to have happened is your ex's lack of trust in your ability to make the relationship a happy one. So, this process involves making necessary corrections and demonstrating to your ex that you are ready for him. You are going to show your ex that his belief that you are not capable of changing was wrong. You will be able to demonstrate that you can change and have changed positively.

Moreover, by the end of this process, you will be able to prove to your ex that positive changes have happened and show him what he is missing by not trying to get back into your life. So, the crux of the

5-step process is to regain lost credibility through introspection and self-talk before attempting to get back your ex.

Step #1: Introspection

The introspection stage is all about getting the right kind of perspective to the process of getting your ex back. In addition to identify what went wrong in the relationship, what was your mistake, and other such questions, you literally need to get inside the mind and heart of your ex to try and figure out what he could be thinking.

You start the introspection phase by getting rid of two commonly abused misconceptions (used as reasons) from your mind, namely:

Your ex broke up with you because you did or said something he did not like.

Your ex broke up with you because he found someone sexier and better than you.

Both relationship experts and counselors find many women who come to them with one or both of the above preconceived ideas deeply embedded in their minds, hoping to get their ex back. You must get rid of these misconceptions from your head before beginning your journey of introspection. A solid relationship will not end on something as frivolous as that "your boyfriend did not like something you said or did." A few words can't have that kind of impact *on a strong relationship.*

In the same way, he did not leave you for someone prettier and sexier. Just recall that he was attracted to your seductive and sexy profile initially. If he had not liked your looks, he would not have pursued you and got into a good relationship with you. Therefore, first, eliminate needless and limiting misconceptions from your head.

This introspection stage includes delving into the details of past conflicts and arguments, the actual breakup and the final trigger for it, and the ideas for the future of your relationship. To do this as well as to be able to follow your ex's mind right through the recovery and getting back process, you need to consider the 360-degree approach, which will give you insights into both sides of all the conflicts in your relationship.

The introspection step should consider each other's childhood, fears and insecurities, educational background, past romances, and dreams and aspirations. Only when you consider all these items, will you be able to assess what went wrong in your relationship. You will also get to know your ex's hidden and innermost expectations and dreams, including those he can't articulate.

During the introspection stage, you must be self-critical and be ruthlessly honest with yourself. Your ego will likely be hurt during this time. You might feel worse about yourself when you are objective and self-critical in your outlook. But, it is vital that you set aside your ego and pride and look at everything through a critical lens to figure what went wrong and what pushed both of you to behave the way you did and why the breakup happened.

These struggles are part and parcel of the process of getting your ex back, and there's little you can do about it except accept it as the way forward knowing that this tough phase will give way to a beautiful end.

The thing to be wary of and be forewarned about is that during this stage of introspection, it is likely that you encounter and realize issues about yourself and your ex that go deeper than the relationship and the breakup. These unexpected issues can be quite overwhelming, leaving you floundering your way through a seeming mess of emotions, conflicts, and misunderstandings. You might even believe that you are powerless to do anything about certain things.

At this point, you must be brave and not succumb to these fears and panic attacks. Instead, find ways to address these hitherto hidden issues head-on. Sooner than later, you will find yourself empowered through the little successes that you will meet. The trick is in building your confidence and willpower to face and challenge your shortcomings and engage yourself in the process of change.

Here are some valid, sensible, and possible reasons for the breakdown of your relationship:

Your boyfriend did not work very hard in the relationship - Human beings are strange creatures. We don't value things that we don't work hard for. For example, suppose you were sitting on a bench in a park, and a handsome man came up to you and said, "Hey beautiful, do you want to have coffee with me?" (For the sake of this example, we will assume that this man is not a jerk or psycho, and he is genuinely is interested in you.) You are happy with the compliment, agree to have coffee with the sweet man, and after that, put him out of your head. Why? Because you did not have to work hard for this.

The same property holds good for human relationships too. If you have given a lot to the relationship and your boyfriend did not have to work very hard for it, then it is likely that he does not value the relationship and soon could end up losing interest in you. If you realize this is what has happened during your analysis, then you should typically NOT blame your ex because this reaction is part of the human nature. People with low self-esteem are those that give much more than needed and get far less from their partner.

So, how do you handle this? You don't need to get totally inward-oriented or selfish to counter this kind of attitude. Just remember to be mentally aware and alert, ensuring your boyfriend puts in as much effort as you do to the relationship so that he learns to value what he has got. To remind you again, people value and give importance to those things for which they work hard and end up devaluing things that come easily.

Your relationship was very monotonous - As a relationship endures through a long period, it is common to see a reduction in both partners' efforts to keep the romance actively burning. Boredom and monotony are two of the top reasons for breakups. As a woman, you can keep this romance and excitement alive in the relationship.

For example, during the initial days of the relationship, your boyfriend would have fought against other men so that they keep their eyes off you. But as the relationship progresses and he finds that you are always with him, then he generally loses the interest to fight for you or "protect" you.

You should use the "unpredictability" factor to overcome the monotony. Your boyfriend should often have to think that he must work hard to keep you. This seemingly unpredictable behavior not only keeps out monotony from your relationship but also gives your boyfriend enough opportunities to work hard, which, in turn, will make him realize the value of it.

Also, when your boyfriend works hard to keep the relationship going, don't forget to add a word of praise or appreciation. Like women, men also love getting compliments and require validation from their partners to feel good about themselves. When this validation comes during a period of monotony, then it boosts bonding between partners and keeps alive romance and excitement that appeared to have gotten lost.

Another way that this relationship could have become monotonous is if unwittingly, you neglected the needs of your boyfriend. Your career or some other aspect of your life could have consumed you so much that you had no time or energy for your boyfriend. Monotony would have crept in without your knowledge because you did not see the fact that you had taken your boyfriend and the relationship for granted.

Your behavior displayed insecurity-driven neediness - Insecurity and neediness are two of the top elements with the power to kill any relationship. Regardless of the strength of the relationship, most men tend to run if they see even the slightest sign of clinginess in their partner.

So, be wary of your validation-seeking needs and ensure your boyfriend does not see them often. If he sees you as someone who wants compliments and validation for every action you take, then he is more likely to see you as his sister instead of his girlfriend. Would he want to have a relationship with his sister? No, right? He is likely to leave you.

Another reason for your neediness and clinginess could have been that you loved your boyfriend so much that unwittingly you fell into the trap of emotional dependence. In other words, you allowed your boyfriend to become the *sole reason* for your happiness; no one else, nothing else. Did you cut off all social contacts? Did you constantly want your boyfriend to spend time with you because you have stopped living your former life? Did you become so obsessed with your boyfriend that you refused to let him do anything alone or with his male buddies? If the answer to any of these questions is yes, then your boyfriend could have easily got scared and run away.

This kind of clingy behavior drives men into thinking that women are a burden. Instead of valuing your efforts in keeping the relationship going, he will think you are a pain, and there is nothing left in the relationship. He will start seeing you as a liability; no one wants a liability in their life, right?

Remember to live your life independently and handle your routine stresses on your own. Avoid leaning on your boyfriend for every small need and problem of yours. Excessive dependence kills a relationship because men are generally not very good at managing emotional baggage, not theirs, and certainly not someone else's.

You were overly tough and rigid - Being excessively tough and rigid can drive away men like nothing else. Rigidity kills relationships and can drive your boyfriend to other women who seek his protection. You must balance independence and freedom delicately in front of your boyfriend.

Men like to have independent women with certain vulnerabilities for which they need the protection of men. Therefore, be wary of displaying too much of strength and independence that could make your boyfriend feel that he is not adding any value to the relationship. "Protecting" his woman is an ancient thought that has not left the genetic makeup of a man since time immemorial.

Breakups don't usually happen because he found someone prettier and sexier than you. Reasons for breakups go deeper than only physical attraction. During the introspection phase, ask yourself this important question and write down the answers for it. *What kind of person were you at the start of the relationship, and what are the changes that have taken place since then?*

The person you were at the initial stages of the relationship is who your boyfriend fell in love with. The changes in your personality and behavioral traits are also probably the reason behind the breakup. See if you can connect these changes with the reasons mentioned in this section. Most likely, the changes will fit into one or more of the reasons discussed here.

Your boyfriend left you not because he found someone prettier and sexier than you but because he believed that you had lost the ability to bring happiness and joy into the relationship. This feeling could not have happened overnight; it took time, with feelings accumulating over a period. Remember, a single action or word does not end a relationship. You must dig deeper and find out the real reasons for the breakup. And for that, you need to spend time on introspection, using techniques like journaling to try and understand the psychology of your boyfriend, yourself, and that of the relationship.

Once you have clearly understood the underlying reasons for the breakup, you can start working on getting your ex back.

Step #2: The Radio Silence Technique

So, you know why the breakup happened after your intense period of introspection. It is now time to prepare yourself for a difficult period ahead. If you want your ex back in your life, then this is the first difficult step wherein you will have to end all contact with your boyfriend. Referred to as the radio silence technique, this step involves completing losing contact with your ex for a minimum of 21 days.

The purpose of the radio silence technique is to help both of you heal from the wounds of the breakup. If, for example, your ex was an alcohol addict, then how do you plan to help him? By first going cold turkey, right? The no-contact or period of radio silence is exactly this.

This seemingly cruel step is essential for the process of getting your ex back to start correctly. Regardless of how painful this is going to be or how much you miss him, you must stick to this step diligently because this step has no exception to the rule. It is a powerful psychological mechanism and has proven to work successfully on numerous occasions.

You will not make even an iota of an effort to contact your ex during this period. However, if he contacts you, then it means you are on the right track. This scenario will be taken up later for discussion. For now, let us look at why the radio silence technique should be followed without fail.

You don't look needy and clingy - Just as a recall, clinginess, and neediness are two of the most prominent reasons for breakups to happen. A no-contact period will make you look less needy and clingy than you did before the breakup. Your ex-boyfriend will realize his folly of thinking that you were needy and dependent on him for everything. When you learn to live your life without the need of your ex, he will remove the label of insecurity and clinginess from your identity.

It creates a sense of loss for your ex - Let us not forget that while you may have appeared clingy and needy, your presence in his life created meaning of some sort for your ex. The no-contact period will drive home the point of losing your love, affection, attention, and presence in his life.

Moreover, he will expect you to call and make contact, and when you don't do it, psychologically speaking, you are playing tricks on his mind. He will start second-guessing his choice of leaving you. These doubts in your ex's mind are the beginning of your success story.

It enhances your worth in the relationship - Remember that point about human beings not valuing something we have not worked hard for? That point will find value for you during the no-contact period. In the absence of what he took for granted and "didn't have to work hard for," he will notice what he is missing. Consequently, he will go into his own period of introspection, setting the stage for getting back together.

It gives you time to recover, rediscover, and reinvent yourself - These 21 days without contact will not only give you the advantages mentioned above, but will also provide you an opportunity for recovery, rediscovery, and reinventing yourself. It would be wise to spend these 21 days trying to analyze your relationship, learn how to correct your mistakes, identify ways to improve your communication and articulation styles, and enhance your knowledge about all aspects of how to get back your ex.

And yet, the primary reason for the no-contact period is to prevent yourself from appearing needy and dependent on your ex for your happiness. The days immediately following your breakup is when you are at the most vulnerable position. This vulnerability makes it very easy to appear needier than before and will drive your boyfriend away even further in addition to transferring the power of your decisions and actions to your boyfriend instead of yourself.

This enforced no-contact period will ensure you have little or no opportunity to display your neediness and insecurity. The power of your life will be in your hands alone.

Let's look at this scenario now. Both of you are living together because of children or work, and radio silence is not possible, then what happens? This can be trickier than when you are physically separated from each other. You will have to work very hard to ensure that your unavoidable daily interactions with him do not reflect any kind of neediness or dependence.

Try and avoid contact as much as possible. Stay outdoors and spend as little time as you can with him. And remember not to bring any new person (read "any male friend") to your house. It is likely to be an act of "one-upmanship" which can be counterproductive to your final goal of getting your ex back.

It would be counterproductive to ignore your ex or avoid him altogether. This attitude might look like you are trying very hard without him and that you are resentful and angry, a situation that is bound to drive your ex away. Look cheerful and happy when you interact when he is around without appearing needy and dependent. Dress well, go out and meet friends, and be happy. The trick is to keep a balance and to show your ex that you don't need your ex to be happy. If staying together is getting to be very difficult for you, then see if you can move in with a girlfriend for a while.

So, what does no-contact mean? It means:

• No text messages or phone calls

• No going over to his house

• No bumping into him "accidentally" at some party

• No contact through any social media platform

• No contact through any mutual friend

The radio silence technique is not just beneficial for you but also useful for your ex. If he has broken up with you, then he needs some space for himself to come to terms with his thoughts, ideas, and his choices. He needs the time and right environment to put things in perspective so that he can realize the value of the relationship that he has called quits.

The best thing that can happen regarding your ex is that he will realize his folly and truly value your place in his life. Consequently, when both of you decide to get together again, there is complete and unmitigated acceptance from his side.

The worst thing that can happen is your ex will be really surprised that you don't need him to lead a happy life. When he notices that you haven't reached out to him, he will start wondering what you've been up to. Either way, the odds that when the time to get together approaches closer, then he will be more receptive to listen to what you have to say, thanks to the space you gave him during the radio silence period.

Step #3: Updating Yourself

The no-contact can be one of the most difficult periods of your life. Yet, as you can see, it needs to be done if you want your ex to value you and your relationship. Treat these 21 days as a golden opportunity for self-improvement. Use it to update yourself. Work on giving up bad habits and cultivating good habits. So, what can you do to reduce the pain of the radio silence period even as you use the time effectively to update yourself?

Change your lifestyle and get an amazing makeover - The reason this point is put ahead of others is that it is the best motivation for self-care. Look after your body and mind and work at becoming a sexy, gorgeous woman so much so that your ex will want to do anything to get back in your life.

For this to happen, you must make your body as your best friend and give it the best treatment you can. Don't abuse your body with unhealthy food habits and lack of physical exercise. Adopt a healthy lifestyle. Get rid of all the junk foods in your kitchen and replace them with wholesome, nutritious food.

Avoid anxiety, depression, and feelings of sadness and make sure you bring back the spark in your personality. Diet, sleep, and exercise should be the primary focus during your 21-day no-contact period. Here are some ideas on lifestyle changes that hold much promise in getting you the desired makeover:

• Change your dressing style - Check out the latest vogues in the world of fashion and adopt those that suit your profile. You don't need to spend a fortune to change your entire wardrobe for this. Just put your mind to it and find clothes that you have already and with some additions can result in a big, positive change. Do not hesitate to wear seductive lingerie under casual, formal, and informal garments because you never predict the future. Always be prepared.

• Change your hairstyle - A new hairstyle can alter your appearance dramatically. Visit your hairstylist, do some research, and find a style that adds wonderful value to your profile. You could start small by coloring a part of your hair. See how you feel and slowly enhance your bravery and try the dramatic.

• Give yourself a good, ravishing skin treatment - If you have any skin problems, visit a dermatologist and find solutions for it. Indulge in a massage and/or a good, invigorating facial. Work on your skin tone and make sure you get rid of pimples, acne, red spots, and blackheads. Smooth, clear skin is the start of any beauty skin regime.

• Get a dental treatment - Visit your dentist to whiten your teeth, get rid of bad mouth odor (if any), and other dental issues. Be prepared with a winning smile at all points in time. Your smile will be the first sign to your ex that you are happy without him.

These physical changes are excellent remedies to boost your self-confidence. A well-maintained body houses a happy mind. Be comfortable with yourself.

Identify a hobby - Go back in time and think of the things you loved doing as a child or a teenager. Think of ideas that you had put into the cold storage because you did not have the time and energy at that time for it. Ask yourself what enjoyable activities you gave up for the sake of your relationship. Rediscover and reinvent your hobbies and passions. Some exciting ideas are listed below.

Join a new exercise class - Physical exercise is one of the best ways to beat the blues - thanks to the rush of endorphins. However, instead of sticking to the old walking, jogging, or going to the gym, try something new and innovative like aqua Zumba, aerial yoga, pole dancing, tango, hip-hop, jive, etc. This will get you exercising and keep your mind on something interesting and good for you.

Learn a new language - Learning a new language might start off as a simple hobby. However, it has the potential to make a great career for you in the future, thanks to job opportunities like a translator, interpreter, etc.

Travel - A change of scene could also be a great way to get over the 21 days of pain and agony. If you have been putting off going to a favorite place for want of time, then now is the time. Book your tickets and go.

You could go alone and make this trip as part of your introspection step or plan a holiday with family and friends and distract yourself with fun and enjoyment. A new place is a great way to see the world and your own life in a new perspective helping you with courage and objectivity, the vital elements to get over a breakup unscathed and stronger than before.

Write - Aside from journaling, which should be a mandatory part of your introspection process, see if you can write something that others will enjoy reading. Poems or stories, perhaps?

Join an art class - If you are the creative and arty type of person, then give vent to your talents and join an art class of your choice. Even if you think you are not a highly creative person, feel free to join a class because you never know what kind of potential talent could emerge when you are in your lowest times in life.

Get back to work - If you have always been working, then ensure you don't take a break during this no-contact period. Go to work and get your head into your profession with deeper earnestness than before. Your job will not only help you get a grip on yourself but also remind you that financial independence is an essential aspect of a healthy relationship.

If you had quit your job for the relationship, then go all out and find another one. It might be a little tough initially. But once you recall your talents and skills and get into the groove, you will thank yourself for it. Working in a professional environment using your professional skills will boost your self-confidence no end and give you the impetus needed to move on without your ex.

Reconnect with your old friends - Reconnecting with old friends or family members is a great way to rekindle your life interests. Your own forgotten ideas might resurface. You could be reminded of what kind of person you were before you met your ex. Additionally, reconnecting with old friends and acquaintances will help you avoid a sense of loneliness; as an added bonus, there will be plenty of things to talk about other than your breakup and your ex.

Spend time finding potential solutions for your problems - Another vital element that you must be spending your time and energy resources on during the no-contact period is to explore potential solutions for your own problems identified during the introspection. When you search for solutions for your problems, it means you are taking accountability for your actions - which is the first positive step towards success.

In your journal, make space against each problem you have identified. Fill in potential solutions that you believe will work for you against each of the problems. Use this problems-solutions setup to set goals for yourself. So, for example, if one of your problems is the lack of self-care, then set a fitness goal for yourself and work towards achieving your goals.

Create a "how to get your ex back" strategy - Create a strategy for yourself as to how you plan to get your ex back into your life. By now, you are clear you want your ex back. Take a goal-oriented approach to the plan. Set daily, weekly, and monthly goals ensuring what you intend to achieve at the end of each cycle and how you will know if you have achieved your goal or not.

Take control of the power struggle between the two of you - You must first understand the power struggle a bit more in detail to know its accurate definition. So, what is a power struggle, and is it possible to sustained happiness in a relationship despite the presence of this seemingly ferocious element?

Some relationships manage to find balance without one of the partners imposing his or her will on the other partner and things can remain happy for a while. However, in the long run, this kind of "amiable giving-in to everything" is neither feasible nor realistic. There are very, very rare cases wherein you can see a happy couple and not an inkling of a power struggle between them.

The lack of a power struggle can happen only when the partners are completely disconnected from each other or are so wonderfully aligned with each other that they are both on the same page with regards to all aspects of their life, including raising children, work/life balance, control of finances, etc.

Barring a minuscule percentage of the world population, for most of us, this kind of idealistic relationship in the absence of a power struggle is almost impossible. We are always finding ways to impose our principles and expectations on each other. When life throws its curveballs on us, we don't always find the time and energy resources to think about everything harmoniously. Consequently, conflicts are common in relationships.

Getting your ex back is winning the power struggle between the two of you, at least for a while. No matter how bad this sounds, the reality is that every relationship is about a power struggle between the partners. Valuing each other, love, and compassion are also there, undoubtedly.

However, at some point in time through your relationship, the power struggle comes into play. For the relationship to be sustainable, it is important to give each the power seat - ensuring that neither of you feels less or more powerful than the relationship, although one or the other is going to be more powerful in any particular situation or circumstance. Finding the right balance in the power struggle by prudently choosing when to let go and when to hold on is a vital element to a sustained, happy relationship.

To get your ex back in your life, you need to hold the upper hand in the power struggle. Once he is back in your life, you can begin the balancing act so that your relationship flowers and blossoms.

Don't worship your ex - Don't put your ex on a pedestal and worship him because he is not a god or even semi-god. He is as human as you are and is as infallible as you are. This attitude of putting your ex on a pedestal is a common mistake most women do during the relationship or immediately after the breakup.

It happens because either blind love or blinding emotions take hold of you and your heart and mind. In these vulnerable moments, you profess your love and treat them like your diol. Worse still, during this period of blindness, you tend to lose a sense of your personality. You lose your personal appeal and attractiveness because you are trying very hard to be what you believe your ex wants you to be.

The truth is your ex does not want you to be anyone else but yourself. He doesn't want a woman who says yes to everything he says and does not have the courage and nerve to stand up to him. He wants an independent, happy person who can add value to his life even while he works hard at adding value to his lady's life. He wants a partner and not a devotee.

Finally, remind yourself that getting your ex back is possible and you can do it with a bit of help from friends, family, and perhaps, even professionals. Remember we are human beings and we don't live well by ourselves. We need the help of others to live our lives meaningfully and happily. So, believe in yourself, and don't hesitate to seek help.

Step #4: Reconnection

You are at that enviable position wherein you have successfully crossed two primary hurdles to getting your ex back, namely introspection followed by radio silence. So, now you have identified and accepted the reasons for the fallout, including taking accountability for your part in it. Your ex is also most likely in talking terms with you again. The stage is set to try to win back your ex and re-establish the relationship.

The trick is getting back your ex is not in working smart and hard to get him back but by clearing the pathway for him to come back to you. The heat and intensity you provide for your ex will decide whether he wants to come back or not. Here are easy-to-follow proven suggestions and recommendations for this process.

Don't lose your newly gained confidence - Always be confident of yourself. Remember, you have already worked on this element and built up your sagging confidence levels in the introspection and the radio silence period. Keep this hard-earned confidence at a high level and make sure temporary pitfalls and setbacks impact you negatively.

You must learn to be happier, more confident, and more relaxed than before when you try and reconnect with your ex. Only then can you stand a near-perfect chance of winning your ex back. The confidence you exude is bound to impress your ex, which, in turn, will drive home the point that you are not desperate to get him back. You are not the girl whom he left. You have blossomed into an enticing flower capable of finding joy, even as she adds value to the lives of the people in her life.

Always maintain a calm demeanor - Patience and a calm demeanor are both useful elements in your journey to reconnect with your ex. The slightest sign of annoyance or irritation from your end will be a sign of desperation, and you will go back to square one. This sense of calmness must, therefore, be genuine and not merely a facade to hide the sense of desperation.

Remind yourself that you are the only cause and reason for your happiness, and no one, including your ex whom you love with your heart and soul, can be responsible for your life. Once you take accountability for what happens, then regardless of the outcome, you will be able to face reality and get ahead with your life. If you approach the reconnection with your ex with this attitude, then you will not lose your sense of calmness at all.

In fact, this sense of calmness is like a new lifestyle. It must sustain through your life even after you get your ex back. Get past your sense of neediness and desperation and only when you are ready should you try and reconnect with your ex. Else, feel free to extend the period of radio silence.

A great relationship with your ex should be founded on self-respect, dignity, and honor, and not based on desperate neediness. Build your self-pride and self-esteem through your work and self-worth. This sense of pride you have in yourself will ensure that you don't depend on your ex for your happiness. Your cup of joy overflows, and your ex can partake of this overflowing happiness created by you.

So, treat yourself with respect, and your sense of calm will always be by your side.

Using text messages - Once the 21-day cooling period is over and you have come to terms with the breakup, and you now want to begin working towards getting your ex back, then starting off with simple text messages is a great way. You must take care not to sound silly, desperate, or needy in your messages, and yet, there must be something in them that sparks interest in your ex.

A birthday message should be just that (not to be done during the no-contact period). Do not use it to start a conversation. A bad example would be "Hi, happy birthday, been missing you. How've you been?" A good one would be "Hey, happy birthday. I hope you have a wonderful year ahead." In case he responds to a good example like, "Thank you. How have you been?" Then, your answer should ideally be - and stopped at - "I am good. Thank you for asking."

Here are some pointers for texting your ex:

• Write in a way that makes your ex crave your messages

• He should be excited about receiving a message from you and look forward to the next one

• Texts from you should ideally get an immediate reply

• Write in a way that the initiation of the conversation happens from him and not you

• Do not ever use negativity and sarcasm in your language

• Do not make text hateful or hurtful

• Start texting at large time intervals and slowly increase the frequency of the messages so that your ex feels natural and comfortable with it

Using phone calls - Once both of you have reached casualness with text messages, it could be time to move on to phone calls. Take your time and decide when you want to take this step. It is important not to transition from text messages to a phone without warning and out of the blue. It is best to include a message that could be like a request to call. If he says yes, then call.

For example, suppose you have been texting back and forth, and you are chatting excitedly about something. At one point, your text could go something like, "Actually, I have something to tell you which would be better over the phone. Good time to call?" By this, you are creating a "setup" that has the potential for a phone call. If he says yes, then the transition from text to the phone can have a great beginning.

However, be prepared to get a negative response from your ex. Take it slow and find another such opportunity after a while. Sooner than later, you are likely to see success.

Write a letter to your ex - Instead of calling your ex, you can also use a letter to write down your thoughts. At this juncture, it might make sense to get rid of certain misconceptions about letter writing, especially to your ex. The misconception is that people think it is not a great idea to write a letter to your ex because it creeps him out. Nothing can be farther from the truth.

Letters are excellent emotion enhancers, which means they have the power to connect and build emotional bonds between the writer and the reader, unlike social media posts, which are very non-personal and many times, tersely brief. Additionally, having a long "Skype" chat with your ex at this stage may not be feasible. So, a handwritten, highly personalized letter is a great option because it tells your ex that you value him. Some key points to remember when you choose to write to your ex:

• Don't write with the intention of winning him back with that letter because it is not going to happen

• Remember, your letter should act as an emotion enhancer

• Write your letter after you have built a good rapport through text messages and phone calls

• Make it fun and an "easy to say yes" kind of letter

Here is an example. Suppose your ex had always wanted to visit a historical monument close by because he is a history buff. For multiple reasons, both of you did not get the time to visit it when you were together. Now, you have a day off in the coming week. Use this to create a little note for your ex which would look something like:

"Hey, you have always wanted to visit {name of the historical monument], right? I have a day off this coming Friday, and I would be happy to accompany you. Interested? Ping me if you are."

It is important to note that these kinds of notes (handwritten letters) are likely to be effective only after a sense of casual comfort has set in between the two of you, perhaps driven by a few pleasant text messages and phone calls. Some more samples of letters you could think of writing depending on the state of your relationship:

A lot of comfort has set in - *"Hey, just wanted to let you know that I have been thinking of you a lot these past couple of days. I've come to realize that you are a very important person in my life."* This note is brief and yet enhances emotion without sounding needy and desperate.

An easy camaraderie has set in - *"Hi! I have some great news to share with you. Call me at around 10 tonight, and I'll tell you then."* The suspense element is critical, and that's why you include a time; there's nothing like a surprise to bring some spark into the relationship.

While these are simple notes that enhance the emotion in a relationship, you could also choose to write a letter in which you explain how and why you believe that this relationship is worthy of a second chance. Of course, this letter should be timed appropriately, perhaps, after a successful FIXIT date. Regardless of the length of the letter or note, a handwritten message has the power to touch your ex's heart. So, use it well.

Work on a strategy for your "FIXIT" date - The "FIXIT" date will be the first date you have with your ex after the breakup. It is easy to see why it is important to focus on and strategize as to how you intend to take this element forward with your ex. Balance is the key. While you must plan well for this all-important date, it is also equally important to take it so seriously that your ex feels like you are desperate.

First off, avoid making your "FIXIT" date a therapy session wherein you pour out all your feelings of hurt to your ex. Leave the breakup wounds out of the discussion right now. Remind yourself of the reasons for the breakup and what lessons you learned from the introspection and 21-day no-contact period. Implement those lessons on the "FIXIT" date.

This date should be planned in such a way that your ex feels comfortable enough to say yes to a second date. Emotions of all kinds -except for a good amount of laughter - should be avoided to ensure your ex does not feel awkward. Let it be a short and sweet date that gives both of you time to gauge feelings for each other. A duration of 30 minutes to an hour would be great, perhaps a coffee or lunch date. Let your conversation be on general topics and keep a dignified distance from your ex during the date.

Call your ex for a date - If your ex has already called you for the date, then great. It is a definitive sign that you are on the way to achieving success. However, if he doesn't make a call to set up a date, then don't hesitate to take the first step after ensuring that you and your ex are on cordial terms and the wounds and the pain of the breakup have been left behind.

While making the call to your ex for the "FIXIT" date, it is important that you sound calm, happy, and relaxed. Your voice should not have the slightest hint of desperation. Another thing to remember is to call and not send him a text message. Your voice should sound smooth and ooze confidence. Yet, make sure you keep your tone of voice gentle.

Try calling once or twice. Be prepared to *not get a response from him*. In such a case, give him some more time, and then make another call. In fact, don't call your ex (in case of non-response) for at least one week. This time gap might make your ex curious about why you called, and he might return your call soon.

Please remember that it is essential not to give up trying to get a "FIXIT" date with your ex. Your ex is going to need time to get over the past problems, and you must respect that need. So, keep trying even while you give him space to recover and understand his feelings for you better.

Step #5: The FIXIT Date

Now you are ready for the FIXIT date with your ex. So, how do you know it is a FIXIT date? Answer the following questions:

• Have your text messages and phone calls been positive and engaging?

• Have you spoken about things that both of you enjoyed doing?

• Have you two been flirting mildly through messages and phone calls?

If the answer to any of the above questions is a yes, then your ex could be keen on rekindling the relationship. You called him, and he has agreed to have lunch with you. So, what comes next is to make sure you do everything right for this all-important date; even if it is going to be just 30 minutes to an hour, it has the potential to make or break the journey of getting back your ex.

First off, don't worry about initial awkwardness. After all, it is the first date after a breakup, and things are going to be weird. You can convert this awkwardness into an opportunity by making him laugh or doing something that will help in getting his guard down. Here are some of the things you must keep in mind for this special occasion.

Choosing the right kind of clothes - This step is likely to be quite a challenge. You must dress well and yet remain dignified and not appear over-dressed. Simple, clean, and comfortable clothes should be the focus of your choice. A nice shirt or top - not gifted by your ex - with a well-fitting pair of jeans and sneakers would be a great option.

In fact, don't worry too much about wearing something that your ex might have seen before. That is irrelevant here. Just try to appear casual and comfortable. Of course, you ought to make sure your clothes are aligned with the ambiance of the place where the two of you are meeting.

Remember, the trick is to remain calm, and therefore, don't fret over your clothes. Just keep them clean and simple.

Go for the date with no expectations - Just because your ex has agreed to come out on a little date with you does not mean he is ready to get back together with you. The FIXIT date is also not the right place and time to talk about getting back together. This date is to get comfortable with each other and to get over the initial awkwardness that is bound to be there between the two of you. So, go with no expectations except to have a nice time with your ex.

Use the time with your ex productively and effectively - You must make the most of your FIXIT date. Spend enough time and indulge in the right kind of conversation so that you learn about his likes, dislikes, and whatever else that is important for you to know about your ex. Some things you must AVOID on the FIXIT date are:

• Don't give in to desperate feelings. Don't let your ex see or even get an inkling as to how desperate you are to get him back into your life.

• Be seductive but not overly sexy. Vulgarity is a strict no-no, but you can be sensual and seductive in your approach; the trick is to find the right balance.

• Don't enter the blame-game zone at all and avoid confrontations of all kinds. What has happened is in the past, and there is no reason to bring the unpleasantness to the forefront right now. The breakup was part of the past, and you have learned valuable lessons. So, don't get into any kind of blame game with your ex, not on your FIXIT date. In fact, don't bring up the topic of breakup at all. However, if he does it, then you respond as you deem fit in a balanced way without taking a defensive or an offensive stand.

• Avoid making him feel jealous of your present lifestyle. Yes, you have learned to be happy without him and to take accountability for your own. But, don't make it sound like you are doing all this to make him jealous. In other words, don't brag.

- Don't ask him about his love life. It could come off as being possessive or jealous.

Make the date all about him - Focus on what he wants and steer the conversation to his likes and dislikes without appearing excessively pushy. Your primary focus is to allow him to talk because you have already heard yourself talk umpteen times. Remember to show yourself as the person you were when he first fell for you. Avoid showing him what you had become just before the breakup. This will be a great way to demonstrate to your ex - subtly, of course - what he is missing.

Ending the date on a high note - Keep your FIXIT date short and brief so that you can finish off with a flourish. As mentioned earlier, a date that lasts for 30 minutes to an hour is ideal for such occasions. Exceeding one hour might end up in a situation where both of you don't have anything more to say to each other, considering there are restrictions on the topics you can discuss. Less than 30 minutes might not give you enough to make the best use of the FIXIT date.

A short and sweet date will ensure that both of you are satisfied and happy and ending it with a sense of wanting more of each other. The following line is a good and effective one to wrap up your FIXIT date: *"Thanks for the wonderful time. I hope you enjoyed it too. Hope to catch up again!"*

Most importantly, don't push for the next meeting. Let this date be self-contained. Progress will most likely happen if this one went off well. Pushing for a next meeting is likely to be seen as being desperate.

Remember that if you want your ex back, then humility and acceptance of reality are vital companions. Pointing fingers at him or taking an offensive stand can be a huge put-off. The primary focus of a FIXIT date is to make your ex so comfortable that both your wounded hearts will heal, and both of you are ready to accept each other willingly, happily, and to have a sustained, long-term relationship.

Now, the question is, should you follow up? Yes, you should. But you must take things gradually without appearing to take control of him. After the FIXIT date, give your ex some breathing space before calling him or texting him again. The follow-up conversation should not be about the date but something else. He should not get the feeling that you are connecting with him only to go on dates.

If the response is positive, then go ahead and plan some more dates if he agrees. Try and make the dates as varied as possible. Show him new experiences and let him see how you have worked on yourself to be worthy of winning him back in your life.

And finally, remember that the language of love once learned and mastered is rarely forgotten. Without a single word being uttered, love can transcend caste, creed, gender, race, and religion. Therefore, in the presence of true love, a silly breakup hardly stands a chance.

If love exists in your relationship, then success will be yours. You can get your ex back each time there is a breakup because love is an all-encompassing gift that both of you have given to each other. Regardless of how unpleasant and nasty your breakup was, you can get back together if magical love is present. Just remind yourself to take accountability for what happened and ensure those mistakes are not repeated. Be patient, keep trying, and you will get your ex back for sure.

The time needed to get your ex back might differ from what was explained in the first sections of this part of the book. It could take longer than the estimated time mentioned here. Don't allow the delay to dampen your spirits and love. Keep at it and repeat your efforts diligently, and your work will bear fruit.

Getting Your Ex Back in Special Circumstances

What if he left you for someone else?

Even if your ex left you for someone else, it is possible to win him back. Of course, it might be more difficult than if changes in your relationship dynamics caused the breakup. But the task is not impossible. The biggest challenge would be to handle your own emotions because the image of your beloved in the arms of another woman can drive you crazy. In fact, handling your emotions becomes a vital area of importance in this circumstance.

One of the most effective ways to handle this situation is to pretend that the other woman does not exist. So, throughout the "Step 5" process, ignore the existence of the woman your ex left you for. You are not going to accomplish anything positive for yourself if you focus on her. Instead, channelize your emotions towards productive work and re-establish communication with your ex after ensuring you have done what it takes to correct your mistakes and prepare yourself to change the relationships positively.

While you go through the process of getting your ex back, focus on identifying ways through which you can prove yourself more worthy of his love and affection than his newfound partner. Leverage the advantage of having a shared history with your ex that his present partner does not have. Once you have established a cordial relationship after the no-contact period, use every opportunity you get to subtly remind him of wonderful moments and anecdotes from the past. Use small talk to remind your ex of the great relationship both of your shared.

Remember, the chances of this idea succeeding are very high because most likely, your ex's new relationship is more of a rebound than the sudden discovery of any kind of true love. Sooner than later (with a bit of your help), your ex will realize that the proverbial greener grass on the other side is not always true. He will also recognize the fact that you were not the only person in the relationship to have been the cause of its downfall. Once he realizes his folly, getting him back will be a breeze.

Long-distance relationship

In a long-distance relationship, the biggest challenge for you is the long-distance between you, considering that physical proximity is a huge help in making your ex understand what he is missing. Trying to get back your ex in a long-distance relationship will undoubtedly be challenging. However, the challenges are not insurmountable. Therefore, it is vital to start the journey of getting back your ex with confidence and not being overwhelmed.

In such a situation, focus all your energies on building resilience even as you work at your personal growth and development. Despite the distance, your ex will notice behavioral and attitudinal changes when you choose to showcase your improved and refined personality.

Remember to maintain a cordial and friendly relationship with your ex during the breakup period and wait for the right opportunity to strike. Until then, work on improving yourself. When your ex sees you, regardless of when that happens, he is bound to be excited to see the new you. He will be compelled to put in efforts from his side to regain his lost love. The vital elements in long-distance relationships are patience and *super resilience.*

Getting your ex back the second time around

While everyone endeavors not to have more than one breakup, it is normal for people to undergo the pain repeatedly. That is the power and pull of human emotions, and sometimes, both of you just end up repeating mistakes. Still, all is not lost. In fact, the presence of powerful emotions is indicative of a strong and unbreakable bond between the two of you. You just must keep improving your self-awareness and identifying and plugging loopholes in the relationship to make it happen again.

In the FIXIT date the second time around, you must remember not to bring up the old relationship. After all, you are now trying to prove to your ex that you can make him happy. You must show to him that both of you can get along well with each other, and fights and arguments will not rule the relationship anymore.

It is best to steer clear of the old relationship and create a new order for the two of you. Talk about your new projects and activities. Illustrate to him your active participation in your life, how you have learned to do interesting things, and how you have learned to be happy by yourself. This renewed positivity will drive your ex back to you the second time around.

Finally, don't hesitate to reach out to professionals when you need it. Breakup recovery is difficult, and it is no sign of weakness to seek help. So, go ahead, lean on your trusted friends and family and leverage the power of professional help too, if needed.

SECTION 3: Keeping Him for Good

Many times, even after knowing that the two of you are completely in love with each other, some events take place that puts us in a reflective status. We think that it is important to take a break from the relationship to truly understand ourselves and do what needs to be done to have a better chance of a sustained, happy, and long-term relationship the second time around.

This part of the book delves deep into the undercurrents of your relationship and how best to work together so that you can keep your partner for good.

Now is the time to ask yourself and your partner seriously, "Do we really need to get together? Or was this breakup a universal sign to move on?" If this question is not answered accurately, the chances of staying together are slim.

When you try to answer the questions given in this segment, you must listen to both the logical part of your brain as well as your intuition. However, it is also important to know and accept that the intuitive part of our personality is the stronger of the two. Our intuition is connected to our destiny and is aligned with the universe and our purpose in it. Therefore, when we can truly connect with our intuition, we can live our lives more peacefully and meaningfully than otherwise.

Interestingly, when we feel compelled to stay in a relationship despite it being misaligned, nature normally takes its own course. There is bound to be something that occurs, which drives separation and breakup. This is because the relationship was not aligned with our destiny.

The thing to remember is that if we are trying to control things like saying "I can't live without him" or "I can't be happy without my boyfriend," then you are effectively trying to curtail your destiny through your ego. If, on the other hand, you find the strength and the power to go with the flow, you are likely to find the right path and partner for your life.

Love allows you to let go so that the flow of life continues unabated. Let us take a situation wherein you feel that you really love someone, and yet, multiple problems keep creeping up in the relationship. But you don't want to let go. You need to ask yourself, "Is this really love driving me to hold on, or is it some other selfish act or reason to hold on?"

If it was true love, then ideally, you should find the power and strength to set your boyfriend free instead of holding onto him and creating chaos in both your lives. By setting your boyfriend free, you are effectively setting yourself free. When you let go of selfish needs, you are effectively creating space in your life for the universe to do what is best for you.

Together Again – Now What?

One of the first things you need to do once you get back together is to face the problems that created the breakup in the first place – and face them head-on. It is best done by both of you together. Here are a few questions that need to be answered now that you are together and are planning to keep the relationship going for long-term.

What caused the break-up? - During the introspection period, this question was put by yourself to yourself. Now that both of you are together, you need to attack this question as a couple, working out joint solutions so that you can keep each other for good.

Before that, ask yourselves if your relationship has reached mature enough level that you can discuss even unpleasant things rationally with each other. Both of you must be fine with opening old wounds (knowing the pain might recur) to discuss transparently and honestly to keep the relationship for good.

Why did the breakup happen at all? What was the core reason? Was there an excessive amount of lying and cheating in play? If this is the case, then the chances of staying together are slim even now unless both of you commit to staying loyal to each other.

If, on the other hand, the reasons for the breakup were simple mistaken issues, then how can you ensure these misunderstandings don't happen again. Identify ways and means to set the record straight and work out an action plan together to prevent such mishaps again. Are you ready to forgive past mistakes and move ahead?

Why do both of you want to get back together? - The answer to this question must be clear, transparent, and without the slightest amount of hesitation. If the answer is anything other than "Because we love each other," then you might need to rethink your relationship. Successful and sustained relationships are based almost entirely on love over which other elements like compromises, support for each other, understanding of each other's personality differences, etc. are built upon. Without love, these elements can't sustain.

Do you still harbor resentment and anger? - Be honest with yourselves because resentment is very hard to keep away. If there is even an inkling of resentment, then you must quickly and effectively address that issue before anything else. In the presence of this toxic emotion, nothing can really move forward in the relationship.

Did you get enough time to get over the resentment and anger so that you can restart the relationship without rehashing the past? If no, then maybe this is the time to finish that part so that you can restart on a clean slate.

Are you ready to focus on the future? - If you are sure that you don't harbor resentment, then it also means you are ready to let go of the past and focus on the future. Is this true? Answer yourself honestly. If you only want your ex back for casual sex, then you can nip your dream of a long-term relationship in the bud. You must be ready for long-term commitment and focus on the future if you want this relationship to last for good.

Are both of you willing to make compromises? - Compromises form the foundation of any healthy relationship. For example, if the breakup happened because one of you is a workaholic resulting in the other partner feeling ignored, then the workaholic partner needs to compromise on his or her working methodology. Such kinds of compromises are imperative if both of you want the relationship to last for good.

Were the goals set during the breakup achieved? - During the time of the breakup, you would have set goals for yourself to ensure your personal problems did not come in the way of a healthy relationship. For example, if you were the needy partner, you ought to have worked on yourself to ensure that desperation and neediness did not mar your personality. Have you met these kinds of targets you set for yourself during the breakup period?

If no, then your intention to make positive changes will appear hollow. Consequently, the chances of a long-term, happy relationship with your ex despite getting him back are very low. If you have done what you promised yourself, then you have taken valiant steps to make your relationship a strong and powerful one.

Have both of you seen personal growth and development during the breakup period? - The breakup time was a period of self-reflection and personal growth and development. If this has not happened and both of you have remained stagnant in this area, then you are likely to face another breakup sooner rather than later.

After you have gained personal growth and development, ask yourselves if you are ready to be this new person always. Are always you willing to compromise and give up some aspects of your personal self? If the answers to these related questions are half-hearted, then, too, a lot more work is needed to keep the relationship going for good. If both of you are not willing to give over 100% to the relationship, the chances of failure are high.

Is your relationship worth trying again? - This question should get an immediate and resounding "yes" from both of you. Even a little hesitation means there is trouble that needs to be overcome before taking your relationship further. If it is a resounding yes, then are you ready to resolve problems in the future through amicable discussions *instead of giving up without even trying?*

Let's try to understand how long-term relationships in the absence of love works. Suppose the two of you have had a good honeymoon period and managed to get through the first year of being together despite multiple fights and arguments. What happens? The partners end up telling themselves that one year is up; let us give it another year before deciding on anything. This may go on year after year - driven mostly by attachment rather than love.

What happens with attachment (as against love) is that the ego of either or both partners come into play. One or both of you are likely to feel a sense of "ownership" over the other, driven by ego rather than love. If this is the case in your relationship, then you need to guard yourself against it. Any relationship is worth multiple chances if both partners know for sure that there is love in it.

Are your expectations from each other realistic? - Relationships are not easy, and if the expectations are not realistic, you are only enhancing the difficulty even further. Not only that, unrealistic expectations are a sure sign of allowing yourself to be delusional because all you are thinking of is to get him back in your life, and nothing more. Therefore, both of you must keep your expectations from each other as realistic as possible.

One of the best ways you can gauge the future of this relationship is to ask yourselves if your partner brings out the best or worst in you. If you or your partner brings out your strengths and confidence to the fore, then the partnership will automatically sustain. However, if your weaknesses are what gets exposed in each other's presence, then it is time to say goodbye and find someone else.

Remember that when your life is aligned with your destiny, then you will not have any insurmountable problems to deal with. It is best not to fight this destiny of yours. So, if your ex says, "Hey, something's not right. Let's split." You will feel pain for some time. But, the right thing to do after making your efforts at getting back together is to say, "Yeah, ok," and letting go of him. After all, what must come to you will find its way back into your life.

The one thing that is a clear sign that your ex is not the right person for you is when you are in a toxic and abusive relationship. Your partner could be using physical, emotional, or mental abuse; the *type* of abuse is irrelevant. If you even have the slightest doubt that your relationship is abusive, the best thing for you is to let go. It would be a complete waste of time and energy to cling on to such an individual. Moreover, it could be harmful too.

It might be a good place to warn you that often, women who experience the pain of a breakup normally tend to panic. They choose to remember only the good things that they are going to lose and forget the bad things that happened, which ideally should be sacrificed at the altar of a breakup. A breakup of an abusive relationship is, perhaps, the best thing that could happen to you. Once you are free from his clutches, you can get back control of your life and find someone who is more suited to you and your needs.

It takes two to tango. So, if you are the one putting in all the efforts to get your relationship on track, then it means your boyfriend doesn't value you. It may not be a sensible thing to try and make your relationship work at all. Asking the question of whether your ex is really the right guy for you is imperative and finding honest answers within yourself is even more so.

Don't be afraid to ask yourself this all-important question. Don't be afraid to delve and find honest answers; it's not that you will only find negative answers, you are likely to find many positive answers, as well. The point is that when you ask this question, you are valuing yourself as an individual, and only when you value yourself will others - including your partner - value you.

21 Daily Habits to Keep the Love Alive

You have worked hard and got your ex back in your life. As a couple, you have realized that both of you are made for each other, and it is important to keep the relationship going. The worst thing about any relationship is that it tends to stagnate after a little while, and a lot of effort is required to keep the love alive.

1. Beware of complacency in your relationship - One of the biggest challenges of a long-term relationship is overcoming complacency. It is easy for both partners to fall into a routine in their love life and end up taking each other's love for granted. Consequently, one or both partners stop putting in efforts to keep the love in the relationship going strong.

In such circumstances, things likely begin to go downhill, ultimately resulting in a breakup. The sad part is that there are no magical shortcuts to overcome this challenge except to keep reminding yourself not to get complacent and not to get your boyfriend's love for granted. Let us take the example of a good car. If you did not maintain it well, the car is going to give up on you, right? The same thing holds good for strong relationships too. Keep polishing your relationship like you would your car, and you will be rewarded with excellent returns through unconditional love and support right through your life.

2. Avoid boredom in your relationship - Boredom is one of the biggest killers of great relationships. Over time, the routine activities of life put both of you in a highly busy mode, and you don't have time or energy for each other at the end of the day. Boredom is one of the by-products of a long-term relationship if efforts to keep it at bay are absent. Both of you must take the onus to keep excitement and fun alive in your life. Don't let your relationship fall into a boring routine; get innovative and keep trying something new as often as you can.

3. Always maintain eye contact when speaking to your boyfriend - When talking to your partner, always maintain eye contact. Yes, this simple habit can help in improving relations between the two of you. When you maintain eye contact with your boyfriend, you are effectively telling him that he is your object of attention. Also, it helps you see and gauge the verbal and nonverbal cues that your boyfriend is giving, thereby empowering you to understand his needs better.

This tip might seem easy and silly. However, the daily stresses and pressures of life can make it very difficult. For example, your boyfriend could be saying, "How about a movie this weekend? Just the two of us?" And you are so caught up in kitchen chores or trying to finish an upcoming office project, and it is very likely that you simply say, "Hmmm" without even hearing the question properly. He can sense you are not paying attention, and his efforts at trying to bring in excitement in a small way are lost!

Let us see how the situation would have panned out if you have made eye contact during this conversation:

• Boyfriend: "Hey, how about a weekend movie this Saturday? Just you and me!"

• You (looking up to your partner with your eyes all lit up at the prospect): "Oh wow! That will be great! How about a late-night show after the kids have gone to sleep! We can take our time and get a drink on the way back! I would have also gotten time to finish an important task related to this project by then."

• Boyfriend: "Whoa! That's what I call a great idea for a romance!"

Right through the conversation, you have not looked away from each other, and the joy of romantic bonding over a movie and a drink can be seen in each other's eyes, which is more than enough to rekindle love in your life.

4. Take trips together as often as you can - Take a short trip away to beat the daily routine whenever you can. The same house, the same supermarket, the same routine day in and day out, can rob any relationship of excitement and fun. It is important to get away occasionally on short trips to other places.

In addition to being together, the idea of looking forward to something you have planned can also add excitement in your life. A nice, short trip helps you feel rejuvenated and invigorated, ready to take on the challenges of life with added gusto.

Also, try and make it a point to go on at least one long trip once a year to a romantic getaway. Don't think that honeymoons are only for new and young lovers. Take a second, third, or fourth honeymoon to keep love and romance alive in your relationship.

5. Visit the same places to experience sweet and romantic nostalgia - Leverage the power and beauty of nostalgic memories. Sometimes, you might not have enough places to visit, considering budgetary and time constraints. So what? Don't hesitate to visit the same places you went to and had fun some years ago. While the trip itself will be great for romance, the walk down memory lane will enhance the bonding between the two of you as you relive happy moments together.

6. Learn something together - It could be a new language or a musical instrument that both of you are passionate about. You could also think of doing a college degree together. Learning new skills is a great way of spending time together in addition to stimulating brain cells and creating new neural pathways, all of which are great for sparking excitement and fund.

7. Include little surprises in your life - Nothing like a little surprise for your partner that will spark his interest and make him fall in love with you all over again, right? A simple, unexpected gesture is enough to do the trick. Even a simple "I love you" note in his sandwich box can stir up the romance between the two of you.

The feeling of getting something, no matter how small, can set his craving for you and your love soaring. Another great way to surprise him is to drop in at his office for a cup of coffee or lunch. The thrill of seeing his beloved when he least expects it can be a great turn-on. Also, if he has had a bad day, then the sight of you could help him manage the difficulties. In addition to love, there will be gratitude too in his response to your little but beautiful surprise. Here are some more ideas to surprise your boyfriend:

• Change his alarm to specially recorded messages from you. It could be cheeky, funny, or even sexy.

• Write little notes on the mirror in the washroom. You could say things like "You are so hot!" or "I love you" or "You are the best" or some such thing.

• Clean up his wardrobe, although it might be a great idea not to trash everything you find unsuitable. Just clean it up and leave the things that you think might not be useful for him and allow him to decide what to do with them. You don't need a fight about him, not finding something he thought was valuable, and you thought it was worth trashing!

• Buy him a couple of tickets to his favorite game that he could go to with his buddies.

• Give him a nice, hot massage.

• Plan a surprise date without having to wait for an anniversary, birthday, or any special event.

• Hug him without reason. Men love to feel their women in their arms. While they might not indulge in this act, they feel loved when their women initiate an out-of-the-blue hug.

• Kiss him in public. Many men love it when their girlfriends cling to their arms or kiss their cheeks for everyone to see. They feel turned on. So, go ahead and indulge in PDA or public display of affection providing, of course, PDA rules of the society you live in.

• Invite his best friends and their families to dinner. You could speak to the wives and get a potluck dinner on a Saturday night, followed by a movie.

• Cook his favorite dish to welcome him home from a hectic business trip.

• Fill his car with fuel.

Don't hold back and think of anything that you know will make him love you for who you are and what you are doing for him.

8. Always show appreciation - Appreciation can never go out of fashion. If he has done a great job cleaning the mess in the garage, say it and make him feel good about the hard work he has put in. Let him know that his every gesture and word make you happy, and he matters the most to you. A little light of appreciation can drive away from the despair of darkness from any relationship and keep the love glowing.

9. Make sex exciting and fun - A boring sex life is another common reason for breakups. Your sex life must be spiced up from time to time to keep out boredom from your bedroom. You might be happy with what is happening in your sex scene, but it needn't be the same for your boyfriend.

He might want to try something new and innovative more often. Be open-minded and know that a great sex life not only enhances bonding but also helps you keep fit physically, mentally, and emotionally. Avoid being prudish because that is old-fashioned. However, it is equally important that you are comfortable too with what your partner wants. Here are some tips to enhance sex appeal in your relationship:

• Perform an erotic dance suddenly. Don't worry if you have two left feet. He will love you even more for your efforts to have him in splits.

• Leave a naughty message on his phone with an alarm to hear it as the day ends. He will look forward to returning home and enjoy some exciting sex with you.

• Get into a hot bath together by candlelight.

• Have a private dance in the nude to romantic music.

• Slip under the sheets naked and surprise him when he comes to bed.

While sex is not the basis of love in any relationship, the absence or monotony of this important element can cause undue stress. If left unresolved (and it is easy and exciting to sort out this problem), then the monotony from this aspect can spill over into the other parts of the relationship - driving both of you away from each other.

Communication is a vital element that will end almost any problem in your relationship, including sex-related issues. You can also spice up your sex life with simple ideas such as new lingerie, having sex in a new place or a new position, or something else that you know will excite your boyfriend. The important thing is not to take this aspect of your relationship for granted, making it seem like a routine chore.

10. Be there for him when he needs you - Most men think they can handle all their life problems on their own. Many of them are mistaken about this issue. They need you, especially when they are in trouble in their personal lives. Help him and be there for him during such difficult times. He will appreciate you and value your presence in his life. Love will follow automatically.

---

11. Take his help - Don't hesitate to ask for his help, especially with things that you know he loves to do and wants to help. Seeking his help will boost his ego as well as give you the feeling that he is attending to your needs without feeling clingy or needy.

Men love to feel like a hero to their women. Your man wants to be your Superman. He wants you to create a space for him in the relationship in which he feels invincible. This feeling of invincibility you render to your beloved will come back by making him do things for you by which you will feel beautiful and wanted. So, don't hesitate to take his help. He wants to help when he can.

12. Accept your partner the way he is - Don't try to change your boyfriend. Accept him with his warts and all. He will love you forever for this attitude. Also, don't judge him for the kind of person he is; importantly, don't mock and humiliate him in front of his friends. If you don't like your partner the way he is, then there is no compatibility, and the foundation of the relationship is shaky.

The core of any great relationship is compatibility, which means each partner likes and loves the other person for who they are. Asking your partner to change some aspect of his because you don't like only that part means you are asking him to be inauthentic, which is dangerous for the relationship.

Shaming or humiliating your boyfriend for some aspect of his personality is a guaranteed way of chasing him away. On the other hand, if you find that you don't like him the way he is, then maybe the relationship should not have happened. So, before you commit yourself, make sure you like your boyfriend wholly instead of telling yourself that you will try and change some parts of him to fit your needs. No way! He will run away from you, never to return.

13. Let your boyfriend know that you trust him - Have trust in your boyfriend and let him know it. When a man lives with a woman who trusts him, then the relationship can grow and develop by leaps and bounds. The more you trust him, the more he will love you and show this love in his behavior. Moreover, trust is a give-and-take. It is only when you trust him that he can trust you back.

14. Try to get along with his family and friends - Your boyfriend's friends and family are as important to him as yours are to you. Don't avoid or find fault with your partner's best friends and beloved family members, especially those whom you know he loves heartily.

Try to be friendly with them and invite them over for occasional dinners, parties, etc. The more you accept his friends and family circle, the more he will want to do the same with your friends and family. Consequently, your reputation as a great couple will spread across a wide range of social circles, enhancing both your self-confidence and love for each other.

15. Talk to him about his work, hobbies, and passions - After a hard day's work, your partner will love to give you his thoughts about the day. For that, he must know that you are interested in listening to him. Therefore, prod him gently with questions about how the day went and what made him happy and what made him sad or angry. Lead him to open his heart out to you. This approach will get your partner close to you.

In the same way, get him to talk to you about his hobbies and passions, even if they are topics that don't interest you much. Learn about his favorite topics and surprise with what you have learned. Try and see his perspective on things. Your partner will not only appreciate and love you for this effort but will also be proud of your ability to read up and think on various topics on your own.

16. Show your gratitude to your partner - Let your boyfriend know that you are grateful for his presence in your life. Acknowledge all the efforts he puts into the relationship and thank him whenever you can. Thinking that you are entitled to him, and his services will surely result in a nasty breakup. Use these tips to send feelings of gratitude to your boyfriend:

- *Show gratitude even for seemingly minor details* - Whether he put out the garbage multiple times in a week or simply picked up your dress from the laundry, say thank you to him whenever you can. Don't think that these jobs are minor and assume that a thank you is not needed. A simple thank you from your lips will make your boyfriend feel valued.

- *Reciprocate his generosity* - Be conscious of the things he does for you like cleaning your car regularly or taking it out for servicing whenever the need arises. Reciprocate these acts of generosity and kindness through actions that he wants. For example, thank him for mowing the lawn by cooking his favorite dish or dessert. These thoughtful actions are powerful gratitude messages that keep a relationship happy and strong.

17. Be supportive of his goals and desires - His goals may not interest you. Yet, his value in your life should drive you to be appreciative and supportive of his personal and professional goals. If he believes he can be a great musician, don't roll your eyes at him. Support his endeavors and encourage him in an open, honest way.

If he wants to attend weekend classes to take his love for music forward, don't stall him. Instead, volunteer to do something that will help him go for his classes without having to worry. Don't shoot down every idea of his without giving it your full attention and focus.

If you do find some of his thoughts unreasonable and impractical, use kind and considerate backed up rational counterarguments as to why you think so. This attitude not only shows that you support his ideas but also tells him that you care for him and would not like to see him get unduly hurt.

18. Have a dedicated and sacred couple time for yourselves - The relationship is for both of you together. Children, work, and other social commitments are secondary (important, yes, but secondary) to the relationship. To safeguard and purity and power of your relationship, you must have regular, dedicated time for yourselves as a couple.

This time for yourselves should be focused only on each other. Make sure there are no interruptions in your intimacy, including being tech-free, kids-free, and free from all else except the two of you.

19. Work on your shortcomings and weaknesses - Every individual has problems, *and so do you.* Your weaknesses and shortcomings could wittingly or unwittingly come in the way of a happy relationship. You must work on these, and at the very least, keep their impact on the relationship as minimal as possible.

Also, demonstrate to your boyfriend your efforts at overcoming your weaknesses. For example, if you have a problem with anger issues, then join a meditation class or go for therapy. This approach will help your partner understand and appreciate your mature attitude to life and its problems.

Suppose you have a problem with his mother, and he knows that both of you don't get along well with each other. The visible effort you put in to be nice and pleasant to her will also not go unappreciated by your boyfriend. He will show his gratitude for your efforts in overcoming the challenges of your life with strength, confidence, and patience.

15 Mistakes to Avoid that Chase Men Away

Racking your brain trying to understand why your boyfriend can drive you nuts. Why do some women have the knack of chasing men away from their lives while some others manage to keep happy relationships? What drives men away from relationships? This section is dedicated to giving you some answers to the above questions.

1. Don't be clingy, needy, or jealous - Clinginess and jealousy are easily the top reasons for breakups. Sometimes, when we feel emotionally stressed out, then the need for extra support from your partner is reasonable. However, excessive clinginess and continuous demand for attention can spell disaster for your relationship driving your partner away from you.

A great relationship grows and thrives when two healthy people live together, giving each other space and freedom to each other. It is vital to have a healthy attachment style with your partner and yet learn how to express your needs from him without being *excessively* clingy and needy. Anxiety about the status of a relationship in either of the partners can cause problems. An anxious partner:

• Worries about her partner's love for her and micromanages his behaviors to identify mannerisms and nuances that could indicate the lack of love

• Is emotionally overwhelmed frequently and needs her partner to make her feel secure and happy

• Is highly insecure and excessively sensitive to slights and insults

If you have any of the above problems, then your boyfriend is most likely going to find you needy and clingy and will want to run away from you. Here are some tips to overcome neediness in your life and become an independent woman capable of being loved and wanted:

Increase self-awareness - Know yourself like no one in the world knows you. Self-awareness includes being acutely aware of your likes, dislikes, weaknesses, and strengths. When you know and accept yourself for who you are, then confidence comes following you like a puppy. You know what will help you succeed and what contributes to your failure. This knowledge will arm you to make behavioral changes for a positive impact on your life.

Face your uncertainties boldly - Remember, everyone has uncertainties and fears in his or her life. You are not alone. The ones who appear bold have only found the strength to face their problems head-on instead of running away from them. You need to do the same with your fears. Every time you feel anxious and worried, don't run to your boyfriend first. Instead, sit with your emotions and try to discern between the rational and irrational ones.

Rational worries invariably have solutions you can work on. Irrational worries simply need to be acknowledged for them to be eliminated from your mind. Therefore, sit with your fears, embrace them, and don't react to them impulsively. Remember, emotions are not the problem. Your reactions to them are the root cause of your problems.

Do not suffocate your partner - Regardless of how much you love your boyfriend, you don't have the right to suffocate him with your neediness. Back off, whenever you feel the overwhelming urge to run to him. Spend time alone with yourself and learn to love yourself the way you are. Not only will he appreciate you for this, his love and respect for you will increase multifold.

Learn to trust - The lack of trust is another thing that makes you feel clingy and needy. You don't trust your boyfriend not to leave you for someone else. Therefore, you cling onto him in the hope that he can never free himself from you. Nothing can work better to chase your man away than this misplaced clinging-based hope.

If there is true love, your man will not abandon you. If he does abandon you, then he was not worthy of your love and affection. Either way, trust in yourself and your boyfriend is critical in a healthy relationship devoid of jealousy and neediness.

Trust him enough to talk about the other guys you meet and work with. Don't give him a nasty surprise if he were ever to bump into you when you are alone with an office colleague, maybe discussing an important work-related project over coffee or lunch. Keep your partner updated on such things.

Maintain a healthy balance between asking for help and being needy - Interestingly, your boyfriend also wants to be there for you like Superman, right? So, how to combine these points? Well, the trick is in keeping the balance between asking for help and being excessively clingy and needy. Your partner should know that you can handle your problems on your own without much help. If you do approach him for help, then it means you think of him as your Superman or the go-to man to do things you can't do on your own.

Give him his freedom - If your boyfriend wants to spend a weekend with his men buddies at a fishing place, don't try to stop him. Let him go and have fun. Giving him space and freedom to follow his hobbies will make him love you more than ever and enhance the respect he has for you. Moreover, this kind of freedom can be used by you to spend some quality time with your friends and family or do your own thing.

2. Don't ever stop being you - What happens is that after a couple of years in a strong relationship, you end up, perhaps unwittingly, give up your old friends, hobbies, likes and dislikes, etc. in the hope of aligning everything with your boyfriend. Don't do this, because then you lose your original identity, which was what attracted your boyfriend to you in the first place.

Moreover, by leaving out your personal elements like hobbies and friends from your life, you become needy and cling on to your partner for everything which most men detest and simply can't handle. They run away from you through the form of a breakup. So, don't make your boyfriend the focus of your life. Make him a value-added element in your life, just like how you are one in his.

Regardless of how strong your relationship is with your boyfriend, you still need a life of your own. Keep in touch with your friends and family, whom you were close to before you met your boyfriend. They add a great touch of individuality to your personality, and the sense of neediness and clinginess will not trouble you or your boyfriend.

Also, when your hobbies and activities differ from those of your boyfriend's, then there will be a lot to talk about these things during your time together. You can share the stories of your passions with each other and use each other to bounce off ideas before implementing them. The bonding is likely to increase when both of you have a life of your own outside of the relationship.

3. Don't prolong fights and arguments - Disagreements are great for a relationship because it can result in brainstorming sessions ensuring the best solution can be found for any problem. However, fights and arguments taken beyond a reasonable measure can tire both of you and drive you away from each other. Try and sort out differences as quickly as you can.

If solutions are not emerging for some of the problems, allow it to rest before attacking it again. Allowing some time to pass will let both of you to see the problem when you are in a calmer state of mind than before, which, in turn, will help in identifying solutions. The important thing is not to let fights and arguments control your relationship. The nastier your arguments get, the more you drive your man away from you.

4. Don't nag your boyfriend - Nagging is a surefire way of chasing your boyfriend away from you. Nagging is one of the topmost complaints that most men in long-term relationships have. For women, it is super easy to get into a nagging mode when the relationship achieves a comfortable and secure status.

Unfortunately, what is easy for you is hateful and unattractive to your partner. He feels that you are not happy in the relationship as a result of which he chooses to run away. You might have a valid point to say to him. You must switch your voice mode from nagging to a softer and a pleasanter tone.

The best thing about most men is that they are simple. Using simple and easy-to-understand and straightforward works is enough to get across the message clearly and succinctly.

5. Don't confuse your boyfriend with cryptic talks - One of the biggest fears for men is not being able to understand what their women really mean when they say something which drives them crazy and chases them away from a relationship. Vague statements like "I'm fine" or "Don't worry about it" etc. are frustrated and annoying to hear, especially when he can see that you don't mean what you say.

Don't frustrate him with cryptic talks that compel him to read between the lines. Instead, be upfront and tell him exactly what you think. If you don't like something he did or said, then say so. Avoid bottling up issues because you haven't found the courage to be open and transparent.

Don't expect your boyfriend to read your mind. Expecting him to know what you are thinking without telling him in so many words can be a big put-off. For example, suppose you are upset that he chose to help your neighbor mow her lawn while he put off doing mowing your lawn. Don't sulk when he returns after completing his task because he is not going to remember that he already refused to do your lawn two days ago because he wanted to have a free weekend. He can't understand the reason for your sulking nature.

Contrarily, if you told him upfront that you are upset with him for doing something for your own home while agreeing to help the neighbor with the same task, it is quite likely he will come up with an irrefutable reason for his behavior. Most likely, he found it difficult to say no to that bossy, aggressive neighbor, and hence, meekly consented. In fact, he might turn around and demand as to why you didn't come to rescue him with a valid excuse when she asked for his help. The matter would have been resolved with resounding laughter, right?

Honest and upfront communication with your boyfriend is not only reflective of your maturity levels but also demonstrates your care and concern for your boyfriend.

6. Don't overanalyze everything your boyfriend says or does - The urge to overanalyze is one of the biggest problems that most women face, especially if they fear that the relationship is not going well. The temptation to read and understand every gesture, word, facial expression, etc. of your boyfriend can put him off completely. You watch him like a hawk in the hope of not missing even a slight change of expression or body language.

This kind of over-analysis is a huge deterrent for most men, and they will do a lot to get rid of such relationships. They will find ways to break up with you. After all, it is not very pleasant to have someone micromanage every word and expression you make. Analyzing in such depth makes your boyfriend feel that he is continuously walking on eggshells, and one little wrong move or word can result in disaster. Your boyfriend will hate being in this kind of a stressful relationship.

So, stop overanalyzing your partner if you are doing so and prevent me from running away from you.

7. Don't allow negativity to control your relationship - While being positive at all times is impossible, you must realize that if you allow negativity to control your relationship, you are effectively trying to push your boyfriend out of your life. Occasional bad moods are okay. However, if you are always going to be grumpy in the presence of your boyfriend, he is going to think that you don't like him and will go away.

After all, no one wants to spend time with people who make them feel bad. So, avoid negativity and make sure your interactions with your boyfriend is happy, relaxed, and comfortable. When you are in a bad mood, please do let your partner know the reason for it lest he assumes that he made a mistake even when he is not responsible for your negativity.

8. Don't put your boyfriend at the center of your emotional life - While excessive negativity in the relationship is bad enough, expecting your boyfriend to help you get back your good mood or help keep you in a good mood *is worse.* This kind of excessive emotional dependence on your boyfriend can push him away from you and your relationship.

You can avoid this mistake by ensuring that you look at your relationship as a place where you take in joy for both of you to share and not as a place to draw out joy for yourself. This approach will ensure that you find your own happiness and have an excess of it to be shared with your loved one.

Putting your boyfriend at the center of your emotional needs will make him feel burdened, a feeling that most men don't know how to handle.

Also, don't bring in drama and game-playing into the relationship. For example, if you think that you must act difficult to get to keep him always interested in you, then you are completely wrong. Men prefer non-dramatic acceptance of their love, and any kind of drama can turn them off, and, in fact, make them lose interest in you.

9. And finally, don't chase after him - If your boyfriend likes you, you will not have a shred of doubt about his intentions to love you. He will make it clear and obvious to you that he loves you. Remember that if a man can be with you and does not take it, then it means he is not interested in you, at least not now. So, don't go running after him because he will run away even further away from you.

The reason for that 21-day no-contact period is to demonstrate to your ex that you are not chasing him and that you respect his need for space. Remember that same lesson here too. Don't chase after him so much so that he feels like a hunted animal. Just be who you are, demonstrate your interest and love for him, and be ready to accept him when he realizes that you are truly meant to be his girl for life.

Expecting a commitment before he is comfortable with you, getting excessively needy, and other such "chasing" behaviors can drive your boyfriend out of the relationship. Enjoy the present status of your relationship and live with as much deep engagement as you can with little or no expectations and without compromising on your own individuality. The chances of your boyfriend falling in love with you for life are very high when you can sustain this kind of positive behavior.

SECTION 4: Setting Relationship Goals to Make Your Love Stronger

The final section of this 3-part book is all about setting relationship goals. What do you, as a couple, ought to focus on so that your relationship thrives in the long-term? Use these tips and suggestions to set relationship goals in such a way that the love for each other grows stronger.

What are relationship goals? Well, just like you have personal and professional goals, you and your boyfriend should ideally think of setting relationship goals, including the plan on how you will achieve them. When you work together to achieve these predetermined relationship goals, your bond grows strong and powerful.

Make sure you communicate openly and honestly with each other - Honest and transparent communication is a vital element for the long-term success of any relationship. It is an integral part of a strong emotional bond and a healthy relationship.

When you make the time, energy, and courage to tell each other your feelings, thoughts, and ideas, then the bond between the two of you increases significantly. From a simple "hello" message to an affectionate email or letter, always communicate with your partner and let him know that he is ever in your mind and heart.

Communicating effectively does not mean agreeing with each other even when you don't want to. Arguments and disagreements enhance the bond of a relationship because it offers an amazing opportunity to see varying perspectives of the same situation, which, in turn, opens a wider range of solutions than otherwise.

However, it is important to make sure your arguments and disagreements are congenial and effective. Talking aggressively and being angry during disagreements is immature behavior. Argue your viewpoint passionately but also value your partner's perspective and never shy away from speaking your mind. But, remember to speak your mind with compassion and kindness. If the discussion is becoming excessively heated, then it might make sense to put it off until tempers are calmed down.

Communication is a two-way process. So, if you want the right to talk and express yourself honestly, then you must give your boyfriend the same right to talk and express himself honestly. Make room to accept each other's opinions and ideas.

Understand each other - Each person has his or her own language of love. To strengthen the bond of love between the two of you, the efforts to understand each other's language is essential. Learn to read and gauge each other's body language and verbal communication. If you don't understand something your boyfriend is saying, then don't hesitate to stop and clear your doubts. The power of understanding each other's language and communication techniques is a powerful love bond that can ever help you keep your relationship strong, happy, and meaningful.

Gary Chapman, author of "The 5 Love Languages: The Secret to Love that Lasts," says that love is expressed in five different ways, including:

- Through gifts
- Through spending quality time with each other
- Through words of affirmation
- Through actions of service
- Through physical touch

Each of us has a primary and secondary language of love that we love to use. The language of love you use on your partner reflects your deepest desires. For example, if you are particularly affectionate with your partner, then it means you desire love through physical touch from him.

The reverse also holds good. If your partner expresses his love through words of affirmation, then it means he desires the same thing from you. Observe each other behaviors and mannerisms and understand each other's language of love and make efforts to mirror each other's language of love.

Make the relationship a priority in your life - While you mustn't suffocate yourself and your boyfriend in your relationship by being excessively needy and focused only on it, it is equally important to make the relationship a priority in your life. It requires time and attention for it to grow and develop into something beautiful and sustainable. Schedule regular couple times and make sure there are no interruptions to result in a cohesive bond with each other.

For this, you should ideally create a couple-bubble that acts as a protective sphere around your relationship. So, each time you need to decide, you should check to see if this couple bubble is being impacted negatively. If yes, the priority should be your relationship. Having said that, it also makes sense to talk to your partner if you need to do something that you believe might affect this bubble both of you have created together. Both of you together can find solutions that work individually as well as help in keeping the relationship bond alive and kicking.

Prioritize each other - In a long-term relationship, one of the biggest challenges to overcome is the fact that each partner ends up taking the other person for granted, which is the beginning of the end for the relationship. You get busy with your work, home, and other routine matters so much that you forget the reason for being a couple, namely, *love for each other.* You neglect your partner in the mire of routine life.

Beware of this situation and make changes right from the beginning. For you, your partner and his needs should come first and over everything else, and for your partner, you should be the priority over everything else. Being each other's priorities is a vital link to building lifelong, unbreakable love bonds that only grows stronger with time.

Make time for yourself also - While you must prioritize your relationship in your life, it is equally vital that you prioritize yourself and your needs in the relationship. Make time for yourself and indulge in activities that may or may not have your partner involved. Also, invest your time and energy in people and interests outside of the relationship.

Interestingly, when you feel proud of your personal achievements, then you bring that sense of pride and individuality into the relationship enriching it no end. This approach must be taken by both partners. If either of you gets excessively engaged in the relationship with enough "me time," then the relationship is likely to suffocate.

Build and stay intimate with each other - You must put in efforts to bring in intimacy in your relationship - at least once a week, if not more. Surveys have suggested that couples who invest time and energy in intimacy are far more satisfied in the relationship than those who don't.

Dating is not only for singles in search of partners. It is also for long-term relationships and plays a big role in bonding needs. Keep courting your partner through little, intimate surprises. Don't hold back in the bedroom, either. Designate a weekly or monthly date night for yourself and commit to this unfailingly.

Don't miss out on planning for plenty of fun times together. Indulge in couple games, give sexy surprises to each other, take off on an impulsive short trip, or do anything else that will enhance the fun in your life. Don't hesitate to act childish and silly with each other. This openness is a powerful bond builder.

Do not underestimate the bonding power of a satisfying sex life as a form of intimacy in the relationship. A healthy sex life is not just useful but is vital for a healthy relationship. Women usually crave for security and comfort in their sex lives, whereas men enjoy variety and visual stimulation. Men see sex as a stress reliever, whereas women see it as a stressing factor *if it is relegated to being a chore.*

For intimacy to thrive in a relationship, these differences must be identified, understood, and resolved. Be open about your sexual needs and get comfortable talking to your partner about it. Discuss sex life at least once a week and make the discussion honest and fun. Talk about what is working brilliantly and what is not. Talk about your fantasies and work towards creating a safe and sexy sex life for unprecedented intimacy in your relationship.

Learn and grow together - As you move forward in your relationship, you are bound to learn a lot from each other and from the challenges that life throws at you as a couple. Learn and grow together through each of the phases of life. Don't cringe away from difficulties and pain. Remember to share strength and responsibility and face life as a strong, well-bonded couple demonstrating what the power of two people in love can create.

Support each other's goals and desires, even if they are different. Getting your partner's support to finish your college degree can help in motivating you to work hard and supporting your partner's dream of setting up a rock band with his music buddies will empower him to scout uncharted territories in the realm without fear.

Be there for each other - When difficult times come, then a couple should be there for each other. Being empathetic towards your partner during his difficult time, *either professionally or personally*, enhances the bond between the two of you. It is all about embracing each other's vulnerability.

Human beings are often afraid to show vulnerability for fear of being ridiculed and/or disrespected. Instead, we often end up digging deep graves in our mind and hiding our vulnerabilities there. The thing with this approach is that fear of your weaknesses becoming exposed will always haunt you, resulting in compromised quality of life.

When you and your partner see each other's vulnerabilities and embrace them instead of ridiculing and mocking them, you feel more confident in being open and honest with each other. The vulnerability you show to each other gets you closer together, knowing that both of you have seen the worst in each other, and yet love has only grown - not diminished.

At the end of the day, human beings want deep and meaningful relationships, and for this, all of us are willing to give our best. Therefore, give your best to the relationship and watch it grow into a strong aspect of your life that will be an example for the others in your friends and family circle to follow.

Conclusion

Knowing and accepting that breakup recovery is tough - but not insurmountable - is a great way to end this book. The trick lies in acceptance and then working towards building necessary tools and solutions for past mistakes to prevent recurrence and to take the relationship to stronger and healthier levels than before. Seeking help is the best gift you can give to yourself during this traumatic time.

Go to a nutritionist and/or trainer to bring about positive lifestyle changes. Visit a music academy to learn music. Don't hesitate to invest in yourself to build self-confidence and courage to take back what is truly yours. Also, remind yourself that no difficulty is unsurpassable if we have the right mindset and attitude backed by a deep desire to want your ex back. Learn to be patient and consistent, and you will see success.

Another thing to know and accept is that regardless of how much effort you put into bringing back your ex, and even after using all the tips and tricks given in this book, there are chances that you may not succeed. After all, love can't be enforced. Moreover, the partnership you are in might not be meant to be for the long-term.

Yet, when you feel for your ex deeply, it is difficult, and in fact, wrong, not to try to get him back and keep him for good. Your hard work will never be wasted regardless of the outcome, thanks to the invaluable lessons you will pick up right through the journey that will come of use to you always.

Moreover, for most of us trying to get back our exes, this situation is not generally true. For many of us, the simple and powerful ideas given in this book should help you sufficiently not only to get your ex back but also to *keep him for good.*

The thing about any relationship is that it takes two to tango. If you believe he is lucky to have you, then the fact that you are lucky to have him is also true. He made a choice to be in love with you, just like how you made a choice to love him. Therefore, you should show as much respect and love to him as you expect from him.

Go ahead: begin your battle to bring your ex back into your life. You are bound to succeed if you keep trying. With dedicated efforts, not only will you get your ex back but will also be able to build a strong, lasting, and meaningful relationship with him.

Resources

http://getexboyfriendguide.com/

https://www.withmyexagain.com/guides/how-to-get-back-with-your-ex/

https://www.withmyexagain.com/guides/why-breakups-occur/

https://www.couples-counseling-now.com/why-couples-break-up/

https://www.vixendaily.com/love/guys-deal-with-breakups/

https://www.huffingtonpost.com.au/2017/08/24/the-reason-men-and-women-deal-with-break-ups-differently_a_23159362/

https://www.youtube.com/watch?v=ruPp_tCs-qg

https://myexbackcoach.com/do-you-want-your-ex-back/

https://exbackpermanently.com/is-there-ever-a-good-reason-to-get-your-ex-back/

https://dating.lovetoknow.com/Understanding_How_Men_Think

https://www.oprah.com/relationships/what-men-think-about-relationships-conflict-and-love/all

https://www.lovepanky.com/women/attracting-and-dating-men/how-men-think-about-relationships_

https://www.youtube.com/watch?v=WdYZEqasDWw

https://www.psychologytoday.com/us/blog/meet-catch-and-keep/201910/8-reasons-people-cheat

https://www.healthline.com/health/why-people-cheat#unmet-needs

https://www.youtube.com/watch?v=lLvVwfKDSdk

https://www.youtube.com/watch?v=uZMuk6VIU68

https://theartofcharm.com/confidence/surviving-breakup/

https://www.mindbodygreen.com/0-7610/17-ways-to-take-care-of-yourself-after-a-breakup.html

https://www.youtube.com/watch?v=yoTAoA6nFTE&t=233s

https://www.exboyfriendrecovery.com/sample-letter-to-write-to-your-ex-to-get-them-back/

https://exbackpermanently.com/use-texts-to-get-your-ex-back/

https://torontosnumber1datedoctor.com/blog/6-tips-on-how-to-act-when-you-see-your-ex-a-great-first-date/

https://www.bolde.com/18-things-to-ask-yourself-before-getting-back-together-with-your-ex/

https://www.youtube.com/watch?v=4Q5WWVUeusU

https://www.youtube.com/watch?v=K6TUp-dip1c

https://www.youtube.com/watch?v=jjrOpxa-wfI

https://www.yourtango.com/2019326292/marriage-advice-how-keep-boredom-affecting-your-relationship-your-partner

https://www.lovepanky.com/women/how-to-tips-and-guide-for-women/how-to-make-your-boyfriend-happy

https://www.bolde.com/9-ways-to-show-a-great-boyfriend-you-appreciate-him/

https://www.bustle.com/p/7-daily-habits-that-can-help-keep-romance-alive-in-your-relationship-8887452

https://www.psychologytoday.com/us/blog/stronger-the-broken-places/201505/13-ways-keep-love-alive

https://www.vixendaily.com/love/huge-mistakes-women-make-that-push-men-away/

https://www.anewmode.com/dating-relationships/7-major-mistakes-women-make-that-push-men-away/

Check out another book by Dara Montano

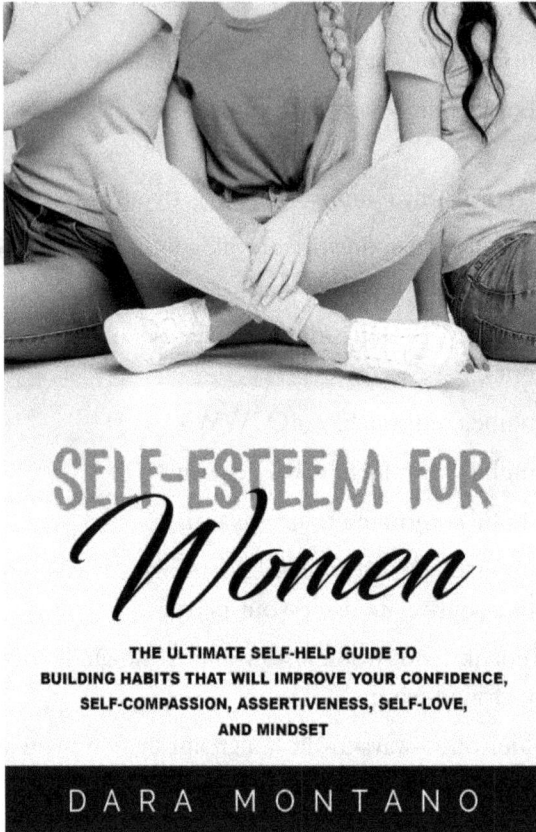

SELF-ESTEEM FOR *Women*

THE ULTIMATE SELF-HELP GUIDE TO
BUILDING HABITS THAT WILL IMPROVE YOUR CONFIDENCE,
SELF-COMPASSION, ASSERTIVENESS, SELF-LOVE,
AND MINDSET

DARA MONTANO

www.ingramcontent.com/pod-product-compliance
Lightning Source LLC
Chambersburg PA
CBHW071954260326
41914CB00004B/798